Holiday club programme
for 5- to 11-year-olds

© Ro Willoughby 2006
First published 2006
ISBN 978 1 84427 204 4
Scripture Union, 207–209 Queensway, Bletchley, Milton Keynes, MK2 2EB, UK
Email: info@scriptureunion.org.uk
Website: www.scriptureunion.org.uk

Scripture Union Australia, Locked Bag 2, Central Coast Business Centre, NSW 2252 Australia
Website: www.scriptureunion.org.au

Scripture Union USA, PO Box 987, Valley Forge, PA 19482, USA
Website: www.scriptureunion.org

Bible quotations have been taken from the Contemporary English Version © American Bible Society. Anglicisations © British and Foreign Bible Society 1996. Published by HarperCollinsPublishers and used with permission.

British Library Cataloguing-in-Data
A catalogue for this book is available from the British Library.

Cover design by Kevin Wade, kwgraphicdesign
Cover illustration by Brent Clark
Internal illustrations by Brent Clark
Drama by Paul Wallis
Printed and bound in Great Britain by Henry Ling, Dorchester

Wastewatchers is printed on paper from sustainable forests.

The **Wastewatchers** website – www.scriptureunion.org.uk/wastewatchers
Visit the **Wastewatchers** website to access downloadable versions of the photocopiable resources and the memory verse song, to read about other people's experiences and check the advice given by other users on the bulletin board.

Wastewatchers is part of eye level, Scripture Union's project to catch up with children and young people who have not yet caught sight of Jesus.

✍ Scripture Union is an international Christian charity working with churches in more than 130 countries, providing resources to bring the good news of Jesus Christ to children, young people and families and to encourage them to develop spiritually through the Bible and prayer. As well as our network of volunteers, staff and associates who run holidays, church-based events and school Christian groups, we produce a wide range of publications and support those who use our resources through training programmes.

To Helen Franklin, whose passion to introduce children and young people to Jesus has inspired thousands to do the same!

With thanks to:
My field staff colleagues, Sarah Bingham and Ruth Wills; Pauline Burdett for her commitment to the families dimension in children's work; Trevor Ranger for writing the song and Paul Wallis for yet another amazing drama; the team at A Rocha, especially David Chandler and Marie Birkinshaw; the holiday club leaders at Wadhurst Parish Church for running a trial of Wastewatchers; Alex Taylor, Helen Gale and Karen Evans for their editorial wisdom and patience towards an editor turned writer; Eric Driver for his horticultural advice and finally, my husband, Robert, whose love of John's Gospel has been infectious!

A ROCHA

Christians in Conservation

The name 'A Rocha' is Portuguese for 'the Rock'. It grew out of A Rocha's first project which was a field centre in Portugal. Since then, more and more Christians have recognised that God has called the church to be involved in protecting creation. Projects focus on science, practical conservation and environmental education. They are cross-cultural and have a community emphasis.

In multi-racial west London, 'Living Waterways', A Rocha's main UK project, is working towards a 'greener, cleaner Southall and Hayes'. A Rocha has partnerships with Lee Abbey in north Devon and with Churches Together in Dronfield, Derbyshire. Local groups in other parts of the UK bring supporters together and more projects are planned. In 2005, A Rocha organised 'Hope for the Planet', a major conference attended by over two hundred church leaders. A Rocha publishes a magazine three times a year.

To find out more about A Rocha worldwide, visit www.arocha.org or to consider becoming a 'friend' of A Rocha UK, click on 'Get Involved!' at www.arocha.org.uk

FOREWORD

Creating **Wastewatchers** has taken many months. It has been a thought-provoking and challenging process and I am grateful to the many people who have made valuable suggestions as the months have passed. The first three chapters of the book of Genesis linked to the whole of John's Gospel form the Biblical basis for the programme. It has been exciting to discover how God's Word has come alive as these chapters have been woven together.

Eugene Peterson (best known for his paraphrased version of the Bible, *The Message*) says this, in his wonderful book *Christ Plays in Ten Thousand Places**:
'St John's Gospel is an extensive presentation of Jesus Christ, Creator and creation, 'at play' in the Genesis creation … Everything that comes into view in Genesis 1,2 is lived out in the person of Jesus among men and women like us and under the conditions in which we live.'

John's Gospel begins:
'In the beginning was the one who is called the Word … And with this Word, God created all thing … The Word became a human being and lived here with us.' (1:1,3,14 CEV)

In **Wastewatchers**, we explore the wonder of God's creation and the wonder of Jesus who is both the agent of creation and yet, as a human being, part of his own creation. We see how disobedience affected everything within that created order.
But Jesus transformed the lives of those he encountered on earth. By his death and resurrection he brought new life to everyone who believes.
We are introducing glorious truths to the children who come to the holiday club. They may understand only a fragment, but God's Spirit (who was also present at creation) will be at work in their lives. They will see how people in the Bible were changed. They will see how those who love Jesus today are changing. They will see how people motivated by the love of God want to change the world. They may be changed themselves as they become God's children.

Never lose sight of the eternal importance of what you are doing in organising a **Wastewatchers** holiday club programme. I hope you too are transformed!

Ro Willoughby
March 2006

* *Eugene Peterson Christ Plays in Ten Thousand Places, Hodder and Stoughton, 2005, p86.*

Contents

Introduction

Wastewatchers is a five-day children's holiday club that focuses on the themes of transformation and the environment. It is based on Genesis 1–3 and John's Gospel and is packed with creative teaching, games, songs, prayers, craft, Bible reading and small-group ideas, along with a drama script for each day. **Wastewatchers** provides a mixture of small-group activity and up-front presentation. The material includes two family services – one designed to launch the holiday club and the other to round it off. Alternatively, these could be used to extend the programme to seven days.

Additional resources are:
The **Wastewatchers** DVD which includes a film in five episodes, the **Wastewatchers** song, the *Learn and remember verse* song, backing tracks, training material on how to build relationships with the families of children in your club and information about A Rocha who have helped develop this programme. Extra artwork is also included. The film is a simple but engaging retelling of each day's Bible story.

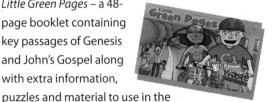

Little Green Pages – a 48-page booklet containing key passages of Genesis and John's Gospel along with extra information, puzzles and material to use in the small-group times. This is ideal for use with 8 to 11s. Eco Sheets for under-8s are available in this resource book. Use these in the small-group sessions and to take home. Both *Little Green Pages* and the Eco Sheets

will help maintain contact with children's homes and act as a reminder, in the weeks after the club, of what the children experienced at **Wastewatchers.**

More information on these resources can be found on the inside front cover. For details of all the resources produced by CPO, see the inside back cover.

WASTEWATCHERS TERMINOLOGY

Bin men/women
The main presenter of the *Wastewatchers* holiday club

The Waste Band
The music group

Taskforce Groups
The small groups that the children will be part of. Activities in Taskforce Groups include refreshment, Bible reading, listening and prayer, games and craft

Clearing the ground
Time to welcome children into Taskforce Groups

On the tip
Time together for Wastewatchers Challenge, Telling the story, singing and praying for the world

Big clean up
Includes quiz, drama, *Learn and remember verse* and light experiment

PART
1

What is Wastewatchers?

THE AIMS OF WASTEWATCHERS

Wastewatchers will help children and adults:

- learn about how God can transform lives
- learn how to hear God through his Word
- learn the importance of Jesus' death and the invitation to follow him
- think about ways in which they can care for God's world
- discover how to campaign with others to bring change to God's world
- build relationships between churches and children's family members.

OVERALL THEMES IN WASTEWATCHERS

Transformation

'Transformation' is the word that unlocks **Wastewatchers**. Children are used to the concept of transformation even though they may not often use the word: a newly decorated bedroom, someone on television experiences a makeover, the changes of seasons, a chrysalis becomes a butterfly.

You might not use the word 'transformation' in the sessions but, as leaders, keep this concept at the forefront of your mind. God (Father, Son and Spirit) brought change by transforming nothing into something at creation (Genesis 1,2). Through Jesus Christ, God transformed the lives of people when there was a social disaster at a wedding (John 2) and when a man who was blind from birth began to see for the first time, both physically and spiritually (John 9). Through Jesus' death, God transformed the broken relationship between himself and human beings (John 19), making it possible for people to enter into a relationship with God, offering his light that gives life. By God's Spirit, Jesus' resurrection means that individuals can receive new life (John 20), while communities and damaged creation can be transformed. All this damage will finally be repaired when we experience the new heaven and the new earth (Romans 8:18–22; Revelation 21).

From nothing to something	Genesis 1–3, John 1
From water into wine	John 2
From darkness to light	John 9
From death to life	John 19,20
From sadness to joy	John 20

> If you cannot do **Wastewatchers** for all five sessions, do Day 1 and Day 4, making sure that the resurrection is included on your last day. Then create the rest of your programme by selecting from the other three days.

Discovering God in the Bible

The core teaching in **Wastewatchers** is based on Genesis 1–3 and John's Gospel. Children will hear stories, read or memorise Bible verses, and learn how to hear God through his Word. These children may forget the leaders and the club but if they have learnt how to read the Bible, who knows what effect that will have years later? During Bible Discovery, a Bible passage is explored each session. Guidelines are given about leading these groups (see pages 28–30). Additional material is provided for older children in *Little Green Pages* (with key Bible passages, information and puzzles to help understand John's message), or the Eco Sheet for younger children after each session outline.

The *Learn and remember verses* are all taken from John. If you only want one *Learn and remember verse*, use John 8:12. This has been set to music, to help the children remember it. See page 17 for details (the music is on page 53). It is recommended that you only use this one verse which is a central key to the whole programme.

Because **Wastewatchers** is largely based on John's Gospel, the way of understanding Jesus' death on the cross is seen from that gospel's perspective. John makes a great deal of the importance of Jesus as the light for the world who knew that he was going to die. He showed up darkness and sin for what they were and are. His death offered light that gives life to those who trust him, as the background story of the snake in the desert clarifies (see John 3:14,15). So **Wastewatchers** does not use the phrase of 'Jesus dying for us as a substitute', because to do so would be to impose concepts that are not to be clearly found in that gospel. Children will grasp from the programme, and from their own use of John, the importance of Jesus' death and the invitation to follow him from darkness into his light.

The environment

Wastewatchers has a background of environmental issues. God created a good and beautiful world that has been spoiled (Genesis 1–3). But part of what it means to be human is to take seriously our responsibilities to the environment, recognising the beauty of God's earth and helping keep it beautiful. As God's transformed children, we have a particular responsibility to care for his world (Genesis 1:27–30; 3:16–19). This theme is familiar to children in modern society. It is natural to move from environmental issues of today into appreciating God's world or vice versa and then to explore the reasons why so much has gone wrong within the world. The environmental aspect of the programme is important. We want children to meet Jesus who can transform their lives. This will affect how they live from now on. The love of God and his Spirit at work in them will motivate them to want to look after and to transform our world which God will finally transform into a new heaven and a new earth.

The issues of justice in a damaged world are closely related to environmental ones. **Wastewatchers** does include some engagement with issues of trade injustice. But this is pursued in more detail in the midweek *eye level* club programme, *High Five*, created in partnership with the Salvation Army, which is a suitable follow-up to **Wastewatchers**. See page 95 for details.

SU has worked with A Rocha (see page 5 for details) in creating **Wastewatchers**. On page 94 there are suggestions to stimulate awareness of green issues in your church – a natural extension of all that has been done in **Wastewatchers**.

If you want to find out more about a Christian attitude towards the environment look at *Caring for creation – Biblical and theological perspectives*, Sarah Tillett ed., (BRF 2005). It includes questions for group discussion and includes many contributions from A Rocha.

Building community

Children belong to different communities – their nuclear family, extended family, school, church and local community. These communities shape the children who come to the holiday club. A holiday club presents many opportunities to build bridges into families and local communities. A suggestion is made after each session about how to do this (Part 4 explains this in more detail). Why not run a community conservation project? Bringing about change in our world single-handed is daunting, but to do it with others is not only more

effective, but can be liberating and great fun! The children's families will also get a flavour of what has been going on at the club. The children themselves may discover something of lasting value about campaigning with others to bring about change to God's world for God's sake!

Team challenge

The key passage for the team is John 1:1–14. This holds all the themes together. A team challenge is to learn John 1:1–14 over the course of the club! Introduce this early on, before team members get tired or preoccupied. Make sure you are all using the same version of the Bible. That may mean that some people will have to relearn verses in a new version!

Families and building relationships

This programme actively encourages the building of relationships – children with other children and with team members; parents with team members and other parents. Children will see Jesus active in the lives of those who are leading the club and in children who already know him for themselves. It is in the Taskforce Groups that this will be especially apparent.

Sympathetic adults spending quality time with children is one of the most precious things we can offer today. Children sharing their faith with other children is also very powerful. We need to provide opportunities to make this possible.

A holiday club also enables the building of relationships between churches and children's family members. This is all about thinking beyond the holiday club itself. How are you going to build on the relationships you have formed? What about the following 51 weeks of the year? See pages 33-36 and 95–96 for some suggestions. *Top Tips on Growing faith with families* (SU) also gives some valuable guidance on this.

DAILY PROGRAMME

This suggested programme allows for 2 hours 15 minutes. Adjust to meet your needs.

EVENT	RUNNING TIME	DESCRIPTION
GETTING READY	45 minutes	Practical preparation Spiritual preparation

EVENT	RUNNING TIME	DESCRIPTION
CLEARING THE GROUND	10 minutes	Welcome the children into Taskforce Groups
ON THE TIP	35 minutes	Warm up Wastewatchers challenge Wastewatchers song Tell the story and/or watch DVD WasteWatcherWord (WWW) Pray for the world
TASKFORCE	50 minutes	Refreshments (5 mins) Bible Discovery (15 mins) Games (15 mins) Crafts (15 mins)
BIG CLEAN UP	35 minutes	The bottle bank Quiz Drama This happened to me Learn and remember Light experiment Creative prayer idea
TASKFORCE TOO	5 minutes	Children to be collected

EVENT	RUNNING TIME	DESCRIPTION
FINAL CLEAR UP	30 minutes or longer	Clear up and evaluate Get ready for tomorrow Lunch/tea together

HELPFUL SYMBOLS

Throughout the book, you will see these two symbols:

All together
Whenever you see this logo, it means that all the children are together to do these activities.

Taskforce Groups
This logo indicates that these activities are to be done in Taskforce Groups

PROGRAMME BREAKDOWN

Each day's programme contains the following elements:

Getting ready

Aims for the day

These are on three levels:

• Practical aims for running this session
• Key truths from the Bible to be understood (God's Word)
• Key truths to apply to our lives (Word for us)

Make sure that all group leaders are aware of the aims. A simplified version is on the Bible discovery notes for Taskforce Leaders (pages 46–47).

The world of a child

Children live in a fast-moving society. Are team members aware of what life is like for a child so they can relate the message of Jesus in ways children understand? You may well have many children who know little about God or have little experience of being part of a church community. Suggestions are given each session to help you communicate with them. Encourage all team members to watch children's TV (without being judgmental) and talk to children they know to remind themselves of a child's world.

Team preparation

The team needs to be familiar with the content of the programme and what they have to do each day. They also need to be aware of issues relating to child safety, leading small groups and talking about Jesus. You need at least two sessions to prepare leaders, which ought to be as compulsory as you can make them. See pages 28-31 for a suggested training programme.

Each session should begin with a time of team spiritual preparation. The mission of a holiday club is essentially spiritual, where children are going to be challenged with what it means to be a friend of Jesus. This is God's work, so it is vital that the team is meeting with God as individuals and as a group. Prayer is not an optional extra!

Clearing the ground

When the children arrive at **Wastewatchers**, they will register and go straight into their Taskforce Groups. During this group time the key aims will be team building, getting-to-know-you and feedback. On Days 2 to 5 this is an excellent opportunity for Taskforce Leaders to ask the children if they can remember the *Learn and remember verse* and the key words for each day. There will be some activities to do during this section, but the main purpose of this time is to talk to the children. This ten-minute section allows late arrivals to join the group before ON THE TIP. Any children bringing pictures or jokes should be encouraged to put them in the bottle bank.

On the tip

This section of the programme is designed to be fast-moving and fun. It contains the main teaching for the day and other elements outlined below. During this period of time the children are all together for the activities led from the front. The presenters of this section take on the role of Binmen/women, confidently steering the children through the programme, but sharing the children's wonder and surprise at everything that is discovered.

Warm up

This is an aerobic workout, giving the children the chance to stretch their muscles in a fun way. It can include simple exercises or a basic dance routine, but should be set to fast, lively music. Be aware of any children with disabilities – if you have a child in a wheelchair, for example, include lots of hand actions.

Wastewatchers challenge

This is a short game played in Taskforce Groups, either involving the whole group or volunteers from each group. A different activity each day should give all the children who want to a chance to participate.

The Wastewatchers song

Make sure you include plenty of music and singing in the programme. The **Wastewatchers** song is available on the **Wastewatchers** DVD, or on *Bitesize Bible Songs* CD (SU). Choose a small selection of songs, including non-confessional songs. There is a wide range of children's praise CDs available; you might like to try *Light for Everyone* and *Reach Up!* (both SU). *Bitesize Bible Songs* is a collection of chart-sound songs featuring Bible verses.

Tell the story

The theme is introduced and the Bible story is told. There is a different way of telling the story given each day. The **Wastewatchers** DVD can be used together with, or instead of, this storytelling method. More information is given on page 27. Whatever method you use, it is essential that all the team listen carefully to the Bible story – the children will watch closely what the adults around them are doing. If you show a love for and excitement about the Bible, then the children are much more likely to engage too!

WasteWatcherWord (WWW)

The WasteWatcherWord reinforces the key theme of the day. An activity is given to help the children discover the WWW. The WWWs for each day are:

Day 1 – From nothing to something
Day 2 – From water into wine
Day 3 – From darkness to light
Day 4 – From death to life
Day 5 – From sadness to joy

Pray for the world

An opportunity for children to pray for others. (There is a more personal prayer activity in BIG CLEAN UP). Let this be driven by the children as far as possible. Remind them that if there is anything they would like to pray for they should write it down and put it in the bottle bank. Remember that people expect Christians to pray so this is not only an opportunity to show that we believe in a God who answers prayer but also show the children how they can talk with God.

Using the DVD or telling the story

The **Wastewatchers** DVD has been created to complement the holiday club programme. This is a simple but engaging retelling of each day's Bible story. Many children will not often watch a DVD with an adult and other children and then talk about it, other than in a formal school setting. Suggestions for telling the story are included. Some holiday clubs show the DVD and then retell the story to reinforce what the children have learnt.

(The DVD also includes **Wastewatchers** and Learn and remember songs, photocopiable artwork and logos. There is also a training feature on reaching the families of the children in your **Wastewatchers** club.)

Taskforce

A time in Taskforce Groups, which will help children and team members build relationships as they have refreshments, explore the Bible, play games and be creative together! Whatever is being done, the Taskforce Leader needs to be looking for opportunities to share Jesus.

Refreshments

Be creative in providing refreshments. Try making shaped-biscuits (bottles, wheelie bins – let your imagination run riot) or something which looks bad, but tastes terrific. This section should allow the children to have at least a drink, and to go to the toilet. Remember to provide for children with food allergies and look out for issues of health and safety.

Bible discovery

Bible discovery is an important time: indeed it is a central part of the programme. We should help the children read the Bible or give them opportunity to hear it being read.

Suggestions for leading and possible questions are given as to how to do this in the Bible discovery notes at the end of each day. *Little Green Pages* (for children aged 8 to 11) is a booklet that contains Genesis 1–3 and selections from John's Gospel, together with puzzles and information. Suggestions are given if you are not using this, but make sure the Bible version you use is child-friendly. The Eco Sheets printed at the end of each day are for use with children aged 5 to 7.

Games and craft

Games can be played in one Taskforce Group, or by joining two or three groups together. Suggestions for each session encourage children to continue exploring the theme. Doing craft, also related to the theme, is a great way to spend time talking with children as you make things together. Remember, while it is great for the children to have something good to take home, don't let doing the craft take over from talking to the children about the Bible story.

Little Green Pages

A 48-page booklet specifically created to complement the holiday club. It contains the Bible passages from Genesis and John that are directly part of the programme and also includes several other stories in John's Gospel where Jesus brought change into people's lives. It is ideal for 8 to 11s to explore the relevant Bible passages in their Taskforce Groups, with puzzles and additional information. It could be used during the club or as a souvenir gift at the end.

Younger children could be given *Little Green Pages* as a gift but the Eco Sheets at the end of each session are designed for them to use in their Taskforce Groups.

Big clean up

During this time, the children are all together for activities led from the front. These activities will round up the day's theme and help the children review what they have heard and learnt so far.

The bottle bank

The bottle bank is where children can put their jokes, pictures, questions and prayer requests. At this point in the programme, select a few items to show or talk about. You might want one of the team to look through them beforehand and select some appropriate contributions. Make sure you have a space to display all the items posted in the bank, so that the children feel their contribution is valued, even if it isn't read out.

Quick quiz

The quick quiz serves as a reminder to the children of

what they have discovered so far. This can be played between Taskforce Groups, but don't major too much on who wins, this is just a quick, fun quiz!

This happened to me

This is a time for you to share your personal testimony. Sharing our stories is one of the most powerful ways to share the gospel with children. There is more guidance on this on pages 30–31, or see the training feature on the *Pyramid Rock* DVD (SU). This will help children see what it means to be transformed by knowing Jesus and what it could mean for them too.

Drama – Park Life

A well-maintained but dull and lifeless park is spoiled by litter. Three young people help the park keeper to restore and improve it along the way by transforming the rubbish into useful things. The drama adds continuity and links to the theme.

Learn and remember

The memory verse reinforces the teaching for the whole week. The verse for **Wastewatchers** is John 8:12: 'Jesus said, "I am the light for the world! Follow me, and you won't be walking in the dark. You will have the light that gives life."' This is also available as a song version on the **Wastewatchers** DVD and *Bite-sized Bible Songs* CD. (The sheet music is on page 53)

Suggestions are given if you want to use a different memory verse each day. But because of the central importance of John 8:12 to unlock the programme, it is recommended that you only have one verse.

The light experiment

The *Learn and remember verse* stresses that Jesus came as light to bring life – a constant theme in John's Gospel. To actively and memorably present this truth, conduct an experiment with plants and light. There are two possibilities and you would be strongly advised to try these out before the holiday club week. The time of year of the club will affect what you can do. Show the plants' progress throughout the week. As with all experiments you need to have a thesis to be tested:

The more light a plant has, the more it grows.

Test One

What you need:

- a packet of lettuce seeds
- at least three pots of soil
- a time switch
- a desk lamp
- a means of recording your results.

What you do:

At least three weeks before the club, plant some fast growing lettuce seeds in a tray, following the instructions on the seed packet. Alternatively, buy at least three plants that are likely to grow quickly.

Label the plants A, B and C and keep them adequately watered throughout. Put plant A in a dark place, B outside, C beside B in the daytime but during the night put it where it is exposed to around 2 hours of additional light from a lamp attached to a time switch. (This will fool the plant into thinking there are two daytimes in a 24 hour period!) Each day involve the children in monitoring the progress of the plants.

> **In the trial:**
> **A** grew 1 cm on the first day, then stopped. By the fifth day, the lower leaves were yellow.
> **B** grew steadily, adding 4 cm by the fifth day but no extra leaves.
> **C** grew steadily but more quickly, adding 5.5 cm and additional leaves were appearing.
>
> Light did give life in that the plants in the light were the ones that grew.

Test Two

What you need:

- a packet of alfalfa sprouting seeds
- three large glass jars, labeled A, B and C
- a cloth to cover the top and elastic bands
- a time switch
- a desk lamp
- a means of recording your results.

What you do:

The day before the club soak the seeds in tepid water overnight. On day one, put the same amount of seeds in each jar, rinse them out, letting the water drain through the cloth. Put all the jars in a warm dark place – follow the instructions on the packet.

When the seeds have sprouted (2-3 days), leave A in the dark, put B on a window ledge and C on a window ledge in the daytime but exposed to additional light as in the experiment above. Each day involve the children in monitoring the progress of the plants.

> **In the trial:**
> All the plants flourished equally until they were taken out of the dark. By day 5, A had still grown but remained yellow and straggled. B and C grew the same amount but had turned green.
>
> Light did give life in that the plants in the light were the ones that became green.

Creative prayer

A more personal prayer time than 'Prayer for the world' earlier. It brings God clearly into the picture and enables the children to respond to him.

Taskforce too

The children go back into their Taskforce Groups before going home. Parents or carers should pick their children up from there – this is a safe way to hand over responsibility of the children and also enables the Taskforce Leaders to make contact with parents and carers. This is an ideal time to chat and finish off craft while waiting for the children to be picked up.

Final clear up

This is time to clear up, prepare for the next session, pray together and even have a meal together. Ensure that you make time to review the session that has just passed. The evaluation form on page 50 will help you to do this.

OTHER ELEMENTS OF WASTEWATCHERS

Wastewatchers environmental project

When you start your **Wastewatchers** environmental project will depend very much on what you decide to do and the availability of the people you need to help you. There are advantages to afternoons, evenings and weekends, so make sure you weigh everything up so that the majority of people can be involved. You should publicise what you are doing so that the children know what's going on and know where to invite their parents/carers/wider families.

The project could be in the form of one already being organised by a local action group for wildlife, the environment or trade justice. New volunteers are usually welcome. Get involved with your local wildlife trust or country park. Consider the RSPB (which is much wider than just birds) or the Woodland Trust Treeforall project. You could contact your local council to find out about sustainability projects. That will show local government that churches are concerned about community issues and want to do something positive to help as well as educating children.

Alternatively you could set up your own project as has been done so effectively in the NOISE, run by Soul Survivor/Soul in the City. Is there graffiti that could be removed, litter that needs collecting, a garden that could be improved for wildlife, trees/bulbs that need planting, a churchyard that needs some attention, bird boxes that need making (to be put up in the autumn), a playground

which is a mess (like the park in the drama)? Are there opportunities for working with Fairtrade groups to increase local awareness, or for setting up a project that could become part of A Rocha's friends scheme? Of course, children are not as strong or responsible as adults or teenagers and need close supervision. Safety issues are especially important with younger children when you take them off-site. (See section 6.12 *Full Day care: Guidance to the National Standards* under www.ofsted.gov.uk/publications for further information on this.)

See what ideas you can come up with. Parents, both those in the church and those with little church connection, may be more than willing to get involved. You may not want to run this during the holiday club/festival but at a later date.

You could even think about running a cycling proficiency course during the week or afterwards. Do encourage children to walk or cycle to the club each day rather than coming by car.

Don't forget to explore other family-oriented activities. For more details see pages 94–95.

Services before and after Wastewatchers

Starting **Wastewatchers** with a church service the Sunday before the club is a good way of getting the church praying for the club and commissioning the leaders. A service after the club will round things up nicely and be a good event to invite parents to. Outlines for these services are on pages 56–57 and 92–93.

Following up Wastewatchers

A holiday club lasts only a short time – what about the rest of the year? How are you going to stay in contact with those children who have no other connection with church apart from the holiday club? Planning follow-up is as vital as planning for the club itself – see page 95. Maybe you could start a midweek club (see page 95 for details of *High Five*, the follow-up programme to **Wastewatchers**), build up links with your local primary schools and offer to take assemblies or to give out copies of *It's Your Move!* to Year-6 children as they move on to secondary school. For ideas and advice, contact Scripture Union on 01908 856170 or your local schools work trust.

Under 5's resources

For details of resources to use with under 5's in your Taskforce Group, visit the **Wastewatchers** website at: www.scriptureunion.org.uk/wastewatchers

Preparing for Wastewatchers

PLANNING WASTEWATCHERS

Ideally, all the helpers should be involved in planning and preparing for **Wastewatchers**. But you'll need a smaller team to coordinate things and make some initial decisions. As well as the holiday club's overall leader this might include your most experienced leaders and your minister or children's worker. Most of the planning team should be taking part in the holiday club itself, but you may want to include one or two who are not, to make use of their particular gifts or experience. The rest of this section covers some of the fundamental decisions the planning team will need to make initially and goes on to describe how to plan in more detail.

Define your aims

The broad aims of **Wastewatchers** are outlined on page 11, but it is important to think about the specific aims that you might have for your club. These will affect the way you set up, promote and run your programme. What kind of children do you want to attract to your club? Will it be a club for all the children in your area? Do you hope to reach out specifically to those children who have had no previous church background (and so present the gospel to those who have never heard it)? Do you wish to nurture the children who are already connected to your church and get to know them better? How many children do you hope to accommodate? One of your aims might be to reach as many children as possible. This will depend on the size of your venue, the number of leaders you have and any financial constraints you have to work under. You may wish to limit the age range – that way you can reach a greater number of a more specific group, maybe an age range of which your church has only a small number. Do you want to use the club as a way of making links between your church fellowship and local families? What are your aims for your team? Do you want to develop the gifts and abilities of the leaders you have available? Is it one of your aims that the club should be a project the church can get behind and work on together? Will the club enable several churches to work together? Can the club be part of the Extended Schools Initiative with churches and schools working together in the local community?

Choose your dates

You'll need to fix the date for your holiday club early enough for people to take it into account when they book their holidays. But you'll also need to take into account other activities that may clash:

- Other holiday clubs in the area
- Other activities already booked at your premises
- Holidays organised by local schools
- Holidays/camps for local Boys' Brigade, Girls' Brigade, Cub or Brownie groups
- Festivals etc taking place in your local area

There will be similar questions about when your potential leaders are available. In fact, the leaders' availability will have a big impact on the duration of your holiday club. If most of your leaders need to take time off work, it may not be practical to run a full five-day club.

Register the event with OFSTED

England and Wales

Normally you are required to register with OFSTED any club involving under-8s which occurs more than five times a year on premises other than domestic premises where the period (or total of periods) in any day during which the children are looked after on the premises exceeds two hours. Even if your club does not fit these criteria, it is good practice to inform OFSTED in writing of your holiday club, so they can keep track of what is happening in their area. Your regional office may give you exemption from registering your event with them if you can prove that you are not primarily providing day care. You may be exempt if:

- the aims of the events are specific and are not to provide childcare
- the main purpose of the holiday club is a recreational activity and subject-based instruction
- the childcare is incidental to the main purpose of provision
- parents or guardians who are present retain responsibility

Never assume exemption; your local OFSTED office will make the decision. For details of your local office, visit www.ofsted.gov.uk. Even if you do not need to register your club, it is still good practice to follow the requirements laid down by the Children Act 1989. Day care providers need to meet the 14 National Standards which include looking at the physical environment, safety, health, special needs, behaviour and child protection.

Scotland

If you are using **Wastewatchers** in Scotland, seek advice from your local social work office. Most social work offices have a community worker, and they are always helpful when it comes to advice about legislation and procedures. With younger children it would be sensible to seek advice and guidance from the Care Commission which is a national organisation.

Choose (and book) your venue

You'll need a venue with enough space for the number of children and the activities you have in mind. If your own premises are not large enough, or you want a neutral venue, you may be able to use a local school or other hall. If you do, try to book it for a few days prior to the actual holiday club week, so that you have time to set up the stage scenery etc. Requirements for accommodation state that the premises should be warm, clean and adequately lit and ventilated, with clearly marked emergency exits. The minimum unencumbered floor space for children aged 5 to 8 is 25 ft^2 (2.3 m^2) per child. Be very careful about large numbers of children in a small hall, and work out the maximum number of children who can attend. The premises you use should meet Health and Safety requirements. Check that the owners of the premises have complied with all the requirements. Ideally, there should be one toilet and one hand basin for every ten children. Disposable towels or hot-air dryers are preferable to roller towels. Smoking should not be permitted on the premises. For more detailed information see *Full Day care: Guidance to the National Standards* under www.ofsted.gov.uk/publications

Insurance

All groups should have appropriate insurance cover. Make sure your club is covered adequately by your church's policy.

Consider your finances

By now you should have a good idea of what your holiday club will be like: where and when it will happen, who will be there etc. But, before you go any further, you'll need to consider your financial resources. First, work out what you'll need money for:

- Craft materials
- Refreshments
- Materials for the scenery
- Photocopying /printing costs
- Hire of premises
- Hire of equipment such as video projector
- **Wastewatchers** resource books for your leaders
- Other resources such as the DVD and enough *Little Green Pages*

Then you'll be able to consider what resources you have. Do you need to do some fundraising? Or will you charge a small fee for children attending **Wastewatchers**? It may be that parents will place more value on a club if they have to pay for it, certainly when working parents are looking for childcare during the holidays. However, this might deter parents who cannot pay. Do what is best for your situation.

Now that you have made the important planning decisions you can start the detailed preparation and administration. Here are the main tasks you'll need to do in the months before your **Wastewatchers** event.

Recruit your team

Make sure you have enough leaders. Your leaders do not all have to be experienced children's workers. Many people in your church will be able to lead a small group of children after some initial basic training. Some will be good at other roles, such as musicians, registrars and refreshment providers. Of course, many of the leaders with these other roles may be group leaders as well.

Adult-to-child ratios

The OFSTED recommended adult-to-child ratios are as follows:

- For 0 to 2 years – one adult to every 3 children (1:3)
- For 2 to 3 years – one adult to every 4 children (1:4)
- For 3 to 8 years – one adult to every 8 children (1:8)
- For over-8s – one adult to every 10 children (1:10) or one in every 12 (1:12)*

There should always be more than one adult for any group and one should be female. **Wastewatchers** is an ideal opportunity to develop and nurture the gifts and experience of the teenagers in your church, in a structured and supervised environment. Bear in mind, though, that helpers under 18 years old (16 in Scotland) count as children and not adults in these ratios. In other words, if you have a number of teenage helpers, you will need more adult leaders, not fewer.

* This is not an OFSTED requirement but is generally recommended. Ensure a risk assessment is carried out and any children with special needs are catered for.

Scotland

These are the ratios required in regulations governing day care up to 16 years of age and early education.
For 0 to 2 years – one adult to every 3 children (1:3)
For 2 to 3 years – one adult to every 4 children (1:5)
For 3 to 8 years one adult to every 8 children (1:8)
For over-8s – one adult to every 10 children (1:10)

Please note that Day Care regulations also recommend that there are a minimum of two adults in attendance at any one time.

* Where children aged 3 or over attend facilities providing day care for a session which is less than a continuous period of four hours in any day the adult:child ratio may be 1:10 provided individual children do not attend more than one session per day.

CHILD PROTECTION

Key issues

The welfare of the children we hope to reach through Wastewatchers is of paramount importance. We are concerned for their spiritual welfare, but also, of course, for their physical and emotional welfare. Sadly, nowadays children are at risk as much as ever before, and it is our duty to do all we can to ensure their safety and well-being as we aim to show them God's love.

All churches should have a clear child protection policy. If you have an established procedure for your church, all of the holiday club team must go through that process. If you don't have a procedure in place, a special club week is a good opportunity to establish one.

The holiday club team need to know who the child protection officer/designated person is and that this is the person they need to talk to first if they have any concerns about the safety or welfare of a child.

The following notes outline the main issues.

England and Wales

Following the Children Act 1989 which came into force in 1991, the government published a code of practice for voluntary organisations working with children called *Safe from Harm* (1993), which contains a number of guidelines for good practice. Most denominations now have established good practice policies based on this and it is important that you work according to the one that applies to you. For further advice or information in the UK, contact the Churches' Child Protection Advisory Service (CCPAS) on 0845 120 4550.

In addition in *Working Together* (2006), the government document on inter-agency cooperation, it states that churches should have appropriate arrangements in place for safeguarding and promoting the welfare of children. Insurers and funders also have the expectation that you have a policy.

Safe recruitment of all those working with children would include obtaining a Criminal Records Bureau disclosure. CCPAS are an umbrella body and can offer advice.

Where working with those under 8 you need to ascertain

if you come within the scope of needing OFSTED registration as a day care provider. Contact OFSTED, again CCPAS can advise.

Scotland

If you are using **Wastewatchers** in Scotland, you should seek advice from your local social work office about registering the group. Most social work offices have a community worker employed with them and they are always helpful when it comes to advice about legislation and procedures. With regard to younger children it would always be sensible to seek advice and guidance from the Care Commission who are a national organisation.

Most denominations now have established good practice policies and guidelines, and it is important that you work according to the one that applies to you. The Protection of Children in Scotland Act (2003) states that anyone working in a 'child care' position must be checked by Disclosure Scotland as part of the recruitment process before they can begin their appointment. Voluntary organisations can register with the Central Registered Body in Scotland (CRBS) to gain access to free checks. Contact the CRBS on 01786 849777 or Disclosure Scotland on 0870 6096006. CCPAS can also advise you.

Northern Ireland

If you are using **Wastewatchers** in Northern Ireland, you should seek advice from your local DHSS about registering the group. Most Social Services offices will have a Social Services Early Years Team. They will help with advice about legislation and procedures. The Early Years Teams have a statutory responsibility for the registration and inspection of all day care services for children from birth to 12 years under the Children (NI) Order 1995.

Most denominations now have established good practice policies and guidelines based on 'Our Duty to Care' and 'Getting it right – standards of good practice for child protection' and it is important that you work according to these. Churches in Northern Ireland can obtain 'Choosing to protect: A Guide to using the Protection of Children, Northern Ireland' (POC (NI) Service). Contact the POC (NI) Service on 028 9052 2559. Details of 'Getting it right' can be obtained from the Volunteer Development Agency on 028 9023 6100.

Appointing team members

Failure to take the necessary steps could lead to a claim of negligence against a church if a child comes to any harm at the hands of someone working with them in a voluntary capacity. 'Harm' includes ill-treatment of any kind (including sexual abuse), or impairment of physical or mental health or development. You should ask all

potential team members to sign a form such as the one available on the **Wastewatchers** website.which gives you permission to carry out a CRB check. Emphasise that it represents positive action for good practice and does not imply any slur or suspicion. Obviously, the nature of the form is sensitive and should be handled with care. Ensure that confidentiality is maintained, in accordance with the Data Protection Act. Do not divulge any information to third parties. If anyone gives a 'yes' answer, allow the individual to explain the situation personally or by letter. If you are in any doubt about the person's suitability, consult your child protection officer. As well as the declaration form, it is recommended that potential team members offer two or more names as referees. Questions to ask a referee might include:

• In what capacity have you known the applicant, and for how long?
• How willing are they to work with others?
• How suitable would you consider them for work with children and young people?
• Are there any relevant details about this applicant which cause you concern?

Never allow anyone to have unsupervised access to children unless they have been through the appointment process. CCPAS advise that all workers are recruited along *Safe from Harm* principles, and *Working Together* recommendations and that CRB disclosures are undertaken.

If you are using parents to supervise children in the community project or additional activities, make sure that they too are covered by your child protection procedures.

Publicity

Once you are confident that you have enough leaders, the next step is to make sure you will have enough children! You will need to publicise your **Wastewatchers** club. There is material available from CPO to help you with this. See the inside back cover for details. Here are some things to consider:

Posters and flyers

Use these to advertise **Wastewatchers**.

Letters and forms

How about sending a letter or invitation card to every child your church has contact with? Or you might distribute letters to all the children in your area, maybe through the local schools. Your letter could enclose an application/registration form to be returned to you. You may also need a follow-up letter, which will enclose a consent/medical form, and perhaps a **Wastewatchers** badge.

School assemblies

You may have a local Christian schools worker, or people from your church who are involved in schools ministry. Or you may have some church members who are teachers. If so, they could promote your **Wastewatchers** event in a school assembly, if the school is happy for them to do so.

Press releases

Holiday clubs provide the kind of story that local papers love to cover. By getting a story in the press, you'll increase the appeal of your holiday club and show that the church(es) involved are reaching out into your local community. By mentioning Scripture Union's name it increases our awareness, which ultimately allows us to improve resources like our holiday club material.

If you have a good relationship with your local press, then make contact in the usual way and inform them of your event. If this is something you have never considered, a press release template is available on the Wastewatchers website. Include your clubs details and send the press release to your local paper.

Prayer cards/bookmarks

It is important to keep your church informed about your event. Prayer cards or prayer bookmarks can help your church members pray for your holiday club – before, during and after your **Wastewatchers** event. You may want to establish a design team to ensure that your **Wastewatchers** material has a consistent look and feel. For example, all your forms and letters should have the same few typefaces, and clip-art should be coordinated so that the style of the various pictures is compatible. Logos should be used consistently in terms of size, position and colour. Logos can be downloaded from the **Wastewatchers** website: www.scriptureunion.org.uk/wastewatchers

Register the children

It is essential that you register all the children who come to **Wastewatchers**. Each child's parent or guardian must have given permission for them to come. You can either send invitations, including a section for parental consent, a few weeks before the club starts, or register the children as they arrive on the first day. You may wish to do a combination of both. (There is a sample of a consent form on page 48.) If you are considering taking photographs of the holiday club you will again need to get parental consent. You should also have emergency contact details for each child, along with any medical conditions or allergies. These should be listed and given to a first-aider. If a child who has not pre-registered arrives at the club without their parent or guardian, send

a consent form home to be signed and brought back the next day. It is important that you record attendance each day, so that you know how many children are present in case of emergency. Each day you should ensure that only the designated adult picks the child up from the club at the end of the session. There is a sample collection slip on page 49. Ideally, you should have a dedicated registration team who will register the children and ensure that they leave the club safely.

Plan in detail

In the few months before **Wastewatchers**, you'll need to consider and organise the following aspects.

Presentation and teaching

How will you adapt the material to suit your particular age group(s)? What audio/visual aids will you need? Will you need amplification or video projection equipment? Who will be the Binmen, responsible for the presentation? Remember, in your club you do not need to use all the material given. Adapt the material to fit your own situation.

Music

Choose the songs for the week, and gather the musicians together to rehearse them. It's good to have a number of musicians playing a variety of instruments, but you'll need to make sure you have enough stage space for other things too! Choose a few new songs and a few old favourites. Make sure you include non-confessional songs, so that the children are not singing words they might not believe. Alternatively, you may choose to use recorded songs and backing tracks. These can be very effective!

Drama

Do you need to adapt the script to fit the number or gender of your cast members, or the limitations of your venue? How much rehearsal time will you need? How will you obtain or make the necessary props, costumes and scenery?

Training

How, and when, will you train your leaders? See pages 28–31.

Craft

Where will you get the necessary materials and equipment? Do you need to ask your congregation to collect particular items (such as junk for the junk modelling)? A dedicated craft team can be very useful, especially in the run-up to **Wastewatchers**. This team should collect the necessary materials etc. They'll also be able to make templates and patterns for the children to draw around or cut out. The craft team should make up prototypes of the crafts, and pass on any hints to the Taskforce Leaders.

Involve local schools in amassing reusable material to use during the week (glass jars, plastic bottles, travel magazines for collage etc.) This gets people actively contributing to the club before it has begun, including the children!

Data protection
How will you maintain the confidentiality of the information you receive on the registration forms? Make sure your church is registered under the Data Protection Act. Visit www.informationcommissioner.gov.uk and click on 'Data protection'.

Games
Consider what games you can play based on the number of children, your venue and the equipment you have. Make sure you have all the equipment you need.

Accidents
Make sure you have at least one person appointed as a first-aider with a current first-aid certificate and access to an up-to-date first-aid kit. The whole team should know who is responsible for first aid. You will also need an accident book to record any incidents. This is essential in the event of an insurance claim. The matter should be recorded, however small, along with details of the action taken. For other health and safety information visit www.rospa.co.uk

Fire procedures
It is essential that the whole team knows emergency procedures, including fire exits and assembly points, and where to access a telephone in case of emergency. Ensure you keep all fire exits clear.

Prayer team
Make sure you have a team of people committed to prayer throughout the preparation and the club itself. Keep the whole church well informed too. The prayer team should keep on praying for the children in the club in the months after **Wastewatchers** finishes.

Setting the scene

Turning your venue into a rubbish tip
The rubbish tip symbolises the theme of the club – transformation of what is a dump into something beautiful. Your welcome/registration area could be beside a large rubbish bin and people responsible for registration could wear suitable clothing. Flowers and attractive plants could appear as the club programme progresses, or pictures of wildlife, or cuddly wildlife toys. This helps establish the theme of the club – transformation.

This area needs to be what it says – welcoming. Your welcome team should be smiling, courteous people! Children need to know they are wanted. Parents need to know their children will be cared for. Responsibility for security begins as the children enter the premises so all administration related to this must be done efficiently. (For sample registration slip, see pages 48.)

The area should be well-marked with sufficient space to allow parents/carers, (along with younger brothers/ sisters) to register the children. Make sure there is space for a queue and places to hang wet outdoor clothes.

Think as well about how you will decorate the Taskforce Group areas. Children's junk models or giant rubbish pictures could decorate the wall(s) beside their area.

Bits of junk could be left around in other areas but you need to ensure that they are not a safety hazard! Do make sure that your venue is brightly lit and warm – but not too hot for the lively games, songs and warm up.

> By the last day in the trial, loads of flowers and plants in pots had appeared at the entrance to the school to welcome the children. Church members had contributed these. A wheelbarrow was a useful, transportable way to move rubbish around.

Decorating the stage
This is a relatively easy set to create, however sophisticated or limited may be your facilities and the artistic skills of the team. The drama script helps develop the idea but you can create a tip even if you are not using the drama. (The drama assumes that you have a park area that is unwelcoming to visitors and then gets messed up.)

You will need a backdrop to disguise the wall behind the stage. Collect old sheets and sew them together to make a large backcloth or make lightweight, portable stage flats by stretching canvas over timber frames. These should be approximately 2.4 m x 1.2 m and hinged in pairs so that they can be freestanding. You will need to weigh them down at the back so they don't fall over. On this backdrop, you could begin with a picture of a beautiful park/wildlife area. This could be incomplete and older children can finish colouring/painting it on Day 1. Alternatively, as the first session proceeds, someone could graffiti the creation images onto the backdrop. This will need to be removed by the end of the week.

On the stage area, begin the week with a small mound of rubbish (which will grow during the course of Day 1 as reference is made to the fall). A variety of large and easy-to-move objects fill the space. Ensure only child-safe objects are used (no used car batteries, glass, sharp edges etc). The tip could be made up of:

- Garden rubbish – branches and vegetable roots are good because they take up lots of space; grass-cuttings are a nuisance to remove!
- Planks of wood, corrugated plastic, bicycle wheels
- Cardboard from large electronic goods
- Scrunched-up newspaper
- Old bits of furniture
- Clean plastic milk bottles

A few things will be removed each day and replaced with other objects that will make the stage area beautiful. (The drama creates a beautiful park with a new pond, a bench and a trellis, that is open to everyone.) The children should be challenged to recognise the changes each day. In the drama, various signs on Day 1 are transformed on Day 5. Whether or not you do the drama, you could create signs that show this change. For example, a 'NO ENTRY' or 'DANGER' sign could be replaced by 'WELCOME' or 'ENTER'. Make the most of your facilities. Think in a multi-sensory way, using smells, bird song, water sounds, certainly sight and even touch.
It may mean that your building will not look as attractive as it sometimes does in your holiday club. Of course, on the first day, you could start out with a beautiful garden and the rubbish dump element does not have to be extreme! Humour and fun can easily be incorporated. But the whole point of this theme is that a beautiful world has been damaged; beautiful lives are being destroyed; relationships with God have become distorted. All this is the result of sin. Symbolically, the ugliness of sin that is transformed by Jesus' death and resurrection is reflected in the transformation of the tip in your venue! Children will not find this strange. Books such as *Stig of the dump* and *The Iron Man* see hope come out of a dump.

> In the trial, an old tyre was covered with silver foil and became a holder of large plants. Other plants were put inside painted tins and other old but decorated containers. A small model bird appeared on different parts of the set.

Using music

Use appropriate music styles for the warm up. CDs of birdsong and other aspects of nature will enhance your programme. Suggestions for using sounds are given for the storytelling on Day 1 and the **Wastewatchers** challenge on Day 3.

Fill the screen

If you are using a video projector or OHP, use a default image while it is not being used so that the screen is never blank. Use something that is simple like the **Wastewatchers** logo or something from nature. If you have Windows XP, this allows you to use your own photos as the screen saver. You could use photos of the local countryside as the screen filler. The logo and other artwork is available on the DVD and on the **Wastewatchers** website: www.scriptureunion.org.uk/wastewatchers

PART

3

Working with your team

DEVELOPING PEOPLE'S POTENTIAL

As well as being a time of great fun and development for the children attending, a holiday club is also an important time for the adults leading and helping out. Helping with a holiday club can be a big step for people in the development of their gifts and ministry.

How does a holiday club develop people's potential?

- It involves people in the church who don't usually work with children
- It is an opportunity for people of all ages to work together in a way that may not happen at any other time of the year. (A regular comment at one holiday club from team members is, "This is the best week of the year in church!" Probably the most demanding and tiring too!)
- It develops people's gifts and lets them take risks
- It discovers people's untapped gifts and enthusiasms
- It provides a structure for the overall leadership of the club/church to seek out and encourage people to 'have a go'. (The age of volunteering has passed so don't rely on issuing a general plea for volunteers. Look at who

you have available and ask people personally, giving them good reasons why you think they could fulfil whatever task you have identified. That suggests that you believe in them! They are far more likely to agree to get involved!)

JOB DESCRIPTIONS

There are a wide range of roles that need to be filled in **Wastewatchers**. The variety of different jobs should allow people to use their gifts. Not everyone will want to present up-front or lead a Taskforce Group, but often there are people who are highly skilled at, for example, providing quality refreshments or welcoming children and their families as they arrive each morning. Some people may fill more than one role.

The Binmen/women

These are the up-front presenters of **Wastewatchers**, taking a lead part during ON THE TIP and BIG CLEAN UP. They take on the role of binmen/women and can be dressed in overalls and thick gloves, carrying a dustbin, rubbish bags or even a wheelie bin, whatever the practice is in your community. They should be confident in presenting the programme, but share the children's surprise when 'new' things are discovered. They control the tempo and atmosphere of the programme, keeping up a lively and exciting pace, but being able to calm things down where appropriate for the more reflective activities. During the Taskforce time they can keep an eye on how things are going, helping team members who have queries or have encountered difficulties. Their overalls make them very visible throughout the session. Having two Binmen/women shares the load and also allows the presenters to play off each other, and maybe introduce some slapstick!

> In the trial, a wheelbarrow was used each day, filled with objects that related to the Bible story, as well as objects that were put on the tip or taken away, as the week progressed.

Musicians – The Waste Band

If at all possible, have a live band to provide your music. This will enable some people to use their gifts where they might not normally have the chance to. Make sure the musicians have a practice and they choose a selection of songs that are appropriate for children from a non-churched background. The band can also provide sound effects for the drama, entrance music for the Binmen and much more. If you can't get a band together, then sing along to a CD player.

Actors

There are four actors in the **Wastewatchers** drama, plus a few extras. Confident actors should take on these four parts. Less confident actors can take on other parts and be involved in the props and set. The 'extra' roles would be a good way to help some actors gain confidence and experience. The dialogue is not complex but the slapstick parts especially need plenty of practice. Children do enjoy the holiday club drama so strive to make it as slick and rehearsed as you can.

Storytellers

If you are planning on retelling the Bible story, either to reinforce the DVD story or in place of the DVD, use your best storytellers. Suggestions are given in each session to tell the story in different ways which involve the children. Decide what works best for your group and makes full use of the skills of the storyteller. Storytelling needs to be practised in much the same way as the drama. Encourage the rest of the team to pray for the storytellers as they tell the story. This is such a key part of the programme so do all you can to prevent distractions or lack of clarity!

Taskforce Leaders

This is probably the most spiritually significant yet demanding role of all! It is these people who will relate to the children most closely and ensure they are comfortable. They will be in a position to answer children's questions, help them engage with the Bible and show them Jesus Christ in the way that they conduct themselves. They are with the children when they arrive, when they are altogether in ON THE TIP and the BIG CLEAN UP and lead the small group times in the Taskforce time. The training of these leaders is very important. They need to know what is going on in the programme but also to be developing their skills in working with children.

Pages 46–47 provide Bible discovery notes for Taskforce Leaders which help leaders know the aims of each session and what questions they need to be asking children, using their own words. These pages are an essential tool for every leader.

For some children, the Taskforce Leader may be the only adult who has shown a genuine interest in them for days. It is vital that leaders are prepared for the rare, but possible, event of a disclosure that a child may make about an unhappy home situation. You must have an agreed procedure for this or for any situation where a child may appear to be at risk. Make sure that all leaders have received some child protection training. CCPAS can help you with both the training and putting together a procedure 0845 120 4550.

Taskforce Leaders must ensure that their own actions are not open to misinterpretation. For example, they should not talk to a child alone in a secluded place. Sadly, touching children is not advisable, although government advice is that a guiding hand on the shoulder or comforting a distressed child would not be considered inappropriate.

Assistant Taskforce Leaders

They share the task of the Taskforce Leader. Young or inexperienced team members are better utilised in this role as they develop their own gifts and skills under supervision. As part of their overall training they ought to receive some feedback on how they have fulfilled their role.

Team Leaders

In a larger club, Taskforce Groups may be organised into teams either on the basis of age or family groupings. A Team Leader will need to coordinate the groups, especially if games and crafts are done all together within the larger team. A Team Leader also acts as support to Taskforce Leaders.

Whoever is organising the games (who may or may not be the Team Leader) needs to do a risk assessment of the games time before the club starts and take steps to minimise the risk to children. Teenage boys are often very good at arranging games! If you have a wide age range, you should consider splitting the children into age groups so that the games are not too rough for younger children. Suggestions for theme-related games are given for each session.

First-aiders

A first-aid kit must be easily accessible and at least one team member should be a trained first-aider. All team members should know who this is and what the procedures are. An accurate record should be kept of incidents and accidents. The parent or carer who registers a child with a specific medical condition should have given information of the condition when completing an application form. Taskforce Leaders and Team Leaders should be informed. Inhalers and other necessary medical equipment should be kept in a safe place.

For more detailed information on first -aid requirements see section 7.7 of Full Day care: Guidance to the National Standards under www.ofsted.gov.uk/publications

Caterers

This team is responsible for preparing refreshments, distributing them and tidying up afterwards. If you are providing food other than a drink and biscuit, your caterers should have a Basic Food Handling Certificate. For more details on how to comply with food hygiene regulations get in touch with the environmental health service at your local authority. Enjoying refreshments in Taskforce Groups is a good way of building up the group, although this may not be possible. Having large plastic bottles of drink and plastic cups makes distribution and tidying up very easy!

Providing lunch or food for the team after the session enables the team to review what has happened, prepare for the next session and enjoy each other's company!

Technical crew

If you are using a full public address (PA) system, with various musicians and presenters, you'll need someone to mix the sound and keep an eye on the equipment. Even in a small club, it's helpful to have someone specifically responsible for items such as TVs, videos or overhead projectors. Someone must take the responsibility to check that the PA, DVD player, OHP etc

all work. If you have fewer than 50 children, you can use one or two TVs to show the video. To link two TVs, you'll need a coaxial cable and a 'splitter', so that the video signal can be sent to both TVs. A video projector is much better, and will be essential if you have more than 50 children, or are using presentation software, such as PowerPoint. (TVs are not set up to receive the type of signal that computers produce, and will not display it clearly.) Either way, the sound will be better if played through your PA system rather than directly from the TV or video projector. The technical crew will also be responsible for cueing the various sound effects, so they will need to rehearse with the actors and presenters.

Welcome/registration/security team

You'll need a team of people to welcome the children at the door, register them and give out the collection slips to their parents or guardians (see page 49). This leaves the Taskforce Leaders free to talk to the children who have already arrived, and the presenters and musicians free to concentrate on the session to come. Once all the children have arrived, somebody should stay on the door to make sure that:

• children do not leave the premises during the club, unless accompanied by the authorised parent/guardian
• anybody who enters the premises has a good reason to be there, has signed in and been issued with a 'visitor' name badge

TRAIN THE TEAM

However experienced your team, there are two key areas to cover in training: good practice in working with children and delivering the **Wastewatchers** programme itself. Here is a suggested programme for two training sessions. They could easily spread over several sessions.

SESSION 1
WORKING WITH CHILDREN

Explore the issues on the next few pages. The more contributions from the team you get the better. So for example, if you are looking at 'Working with a group', invite team members to come up with two key bits of advice they would give to anyone who is going to work with a Taskforce Group for the first time. Write all contributions on a board and ensure that you have covered all the important points. Do the same for the other topics.

Introduce the evaluation form on page 50 as a way of involving everyone and encouraging group and personal assessment.

Working with a group

- Ensure that you get to know each child by name.
- Watch for children who sit on the edge of the group.
- Never assume that all the children will learn from or experience the club in the same way.
- Make sure that all of the children know they can come to you with any questions.
- Be prepared for incidents of any kind!
- Remember that everything you say is listened to.
- For some children, you might be the only adult who shows an interest in them that week.

Behaviour issues

- Set some ground rules and boundaries for the group – and stick to them!
- Have plenty of materials for everyone.
- Ensure that you have enough leaders at all times.
- Positively reinforce the children's behaviour when they answer or do something well.
- Never sacrifice the needs of the group for one child.

Talking to children

- Think about the words you are using – are they easily understood and do they explain the stories?
- Don't talk down to the children – talk with them! This means getting to their level, physically and verbally.
- Let the children express their thoughts and views on the stories.
- Don't always rush to fill silences while the children think of the responses.
- Validate all responses, either by more questioning or by asking others what they think.

How to pray with children

- Ask the children to name some of the things they want to pray for.
- Break these down into things they want to say sorry for, things they want to say thank you to God for, and things they want to ask for themselves or others.
- If you are going to lead the prayer yourself, make sure that you keep to the point and include the suggestions the children made.
- Encourage the children, where possible, to lead the prayers with you.
- Be imaginative in using different ways to pray, eg using pictures or objects to stimulate thought; music to help praise or reflection; prayers with a set response; taking it in turns using one sentence; or prayers using different bodily postures. Suggestions are given each day for praying creatively.

How to build relationships with children

- Be honest with them – children can often see through pretence!
- Be willing and able to share your story.
- React to the Bible story with them; tell them how you feel as part of your exploration.
- Be ready to take surprising responses and comments without being floored.
- Don't pretend to be up to the minute with their lives. Ask them to tell you what's going on and what's new.
- Never be afraid to admit that you don't know something – we are all on a journey of discovery together.

Preparing to work with children

- Think about the activities you are about to do, and allow for the possibilities of mess and difficulties.
- Gather together the resources you will need and have them close at hand.
- Check that the felt-tip pens work and that the paints have not dried out!
- Consider how you will move from one activity to the next.

Reading the Bible with children

At **Wastewatchers** we want children to understand that the Bible is God's Word for them today. It is important that the times when you read the Bible together are enjoyable and make sense to them! Children are not simply reading the Bible to get answers to our questions. Instead, we want their curiosity raised so that they can expect to meet God as they read the Bible, not just now, but in the future.

Little Green Pages is there to help you read the relevant part of the Bible at the club. Make sure that you have a child-friendly version of the Bible with you which doesn't look tatty. (The CEV is the version used in *Little Green Pages*.) If you copy out the relevant verses onto paper or acetate, ensure that the children see that it is from the Bible.

- Break a Bible passage into smaller chunks and go over it a little at a time.
- Think of ways to engage the children's thoughts as the verses are read. Help them listen. Suggestions for this have been given each day.
- Ask only a confident child to read out loud.
- Remember that many children find reading difficult, because of their age and/or educational ability. This does not stop them listening or using their imaginations to enter the Bible.
- This might be a child's first experience of Bible reading. Make it a positive one!
- You will need to explain about chapters and verses. Use page numbers where possible.
- Be prepared to recommend a Bible reading guide to follow up **Wastewatchers**. (See the inside front cover for details of how to find what is available for which age group.)

Helping children to respond

Much of the material you will cover in **Wastewatchers** may prompt children to want to be friends with Jesus for themselves. Be ready to help them.

- They rarely need long explanations, just simple answers to questions.
- Talk to them in a place where you can be seen by others.
- Never put pressure on children to respond in a particular way, just help them take one step closer to Jesus when they are ready. We don't want them to respond just to please us!
- Remember, for many children there are a number of commitments as their understanding grows.
- Many children just need a bit of help to say what they want to say to God. Here is a suggested prayer they could use to make a commitment to Jesus:

> Jesus, I want to be your friend.
> Thank you that you love me.
> Thank you for living in the world and dying on a cross for me.
> I'm sorry for all the wrong things I have done.
> Please forgive me and let me be your friend.
> Please let the Holy Spirit help me be like you.
> Amen.

- Reassure them that God hears us when we talk with him and has promised to forgive us and help us to be his friends. Children need help to stick with Jesus, especially if their parents don't believe.
- Assure them that God wants to hear whatever they say. Give them some prayer ideas.
- Encourage them to keep coming to Christian activities, not necessarily on Sundays – their church might have to be the midweek club or a school lunch-time club.
- Reading the Bible will be easier with something like Snapshots – but you need to support them if they are to keep it up.
- Keep praying and maintain your relationship with them and their families wherever possible.

Talking about what Jesus means to you

So many people put their trust in Jesus because they have heard how important he is to someone else. Team members during **Wastewatchers** have a great opportunity to share what Jesus means to them with the children, and also to show by the way they live their lives that Jesus really is alive! Here are some pointers to bear in mind when you're talking with children about what Jesus means to you:

- Make sure you don't use Christian jargon or concepts that just don't make sense – 'Inviting Jesus into your heart' might suggest to some children that Jesus is only welcome in a bit of them. The idea of a person you can't see living inside your body can be a bit spooky!
- Remember you are talking to children whose experience of life is not as broad as an adult's. Their uncertainties and questions are different from an adult's. Address their issues by referring to experiences which are relevant to them. This is not necessarily just what it was like for you when you were a child! But, for example, the emotions you experienced when you recently changed job may be very similar to those of a child changing school. God was with you then, so can be with a child.
- Speak about Jesus as someone you know and are enthusiastic about.
- Make reference to what the Bible says in a way that makes a child want to read the Bible for themselves – sound enthusiastic about what God has said to us. Tell a Bible story briefly to explain a point.
- Be brief and speak with simple sentences, using appropriate language.
- Be honest, talking about the good and the bad times. God doesn't always give answers or the answers we want.
- It is important to talk about what Jesus means to us now and not when we first came to know him dozens of years ago.

If you are involved in up-front presentation, during the BIG CLEAN UP times, here are some other points to consider:

- An interview process is less intense and invites the children to engage with what the interviewee is saying.
- Include questions or information about subjects such as favourite colours, food, team, job, hopes, worst moments, as well as favourite Bible character or story. Think what a child is curious about. 'Normal' information communicates that being a Christian is all about Jesus being with us all the time, being normal!
- Not everyone's experience will be appropriate, however dramatic it might be! Long and complicated stories will lose children. A group with a wide age range will also affect what is suitable.
- Use someone's story which is relevant to the theme of the day.
- Choose a variety of people with different experiences to share what Jesus means to them over the week.

• It would be worth the team hearing what is going to be said in advance, if someone's experience is going to raise questions that may be a challenge to answer. Whether you're speaking in front of the whole club, or one taskforce group, you should be ready to tell your story, so think beforehand about what you are going to say, just as you would practise music or drama. It isn't a speech but there is no excuse for rambling.

SESSION 2
THE WASTEWATCHERS
PROGRAMME

Introduction

Make sure everyone feels welcome. Then read from John 1:35–42. This is a well-known story in which Andrew meets Jesus and is so excited that he drags his brother Simon along too! Share together what it is about Jesus that excites you and why you would rush to bring children to meet Jesus for themselves. Pray for one another, that during **Wastewatchers** you will have the thrill of introducing many children to Jesus.

Wastewatchers explained

Explain the overall themes of the programme (see pages 11–13), making the transformation theme clear. Show how the personal transformation that comes about when we belong to Christ is balanced by the transformation that we are bringing about as we care for the environment. Tie this in with the transformation of the rubbish tip/park. You will also want to introduce the challenge to team members to learn John 1:1–14. Teach the song and show the first episode of the DVD, if you are using it.

Show everyone the Bible discovery notes for Taskforce Leaders for each session on pages 46–47. These clearly state the aims for each day and questions they could ask, using their own words. It is essential that each leader has a copy of these at the start of each day, so that they can be prepared – indeed, they ought to have had them some time before the club starts so that they can come prepared.

Go through the aims of Wastewatchers

Make sure everyone has a copy of the aims you have already set for **Wastewatchers** (see page 11) and split into groups to discuss them. Are there any other aims that the small groups can identify? This exercise will help you refine your aims and encourage your team to take ownership of them.

Practicalities

Cover health and safety, risk assessments, fire procedures and basic child protection information – if your church has a coordinator for this, they should be able to help at this point. Alternatively, contact the CCPAS.

FURTHER TRAINING

There is a training feature on sharing your faith with children on *Pyramid Rock* DVD. ISBN: 978 1 84427 193 5. To find out more about training offered by SU and for any other training needs contact Alastair Wood on tel: 01908 856044 or email: trainman@scriptureunion.org.uk

WORKING WITH CHILDREN WITH SPECIAL NEEDS

- Value every child as an individual. Before the start, find out as much as possible about them – their likes and dislikes, strengths and limitations. Then you will know how best to include them and make them feel safe.

- Prepare each session with a range of abilities in mind. Think carefully about working with abstract ideas. These may be misunderstood and taken literally! Have a range of craft ideas. Check that you do not give a child with learning difficulties a task that is appropriate for their reading age but inappropriate for their actual age. In other words, make sure that pictures and other aids are age-appropriate.

- Give all children opportunities to join in activities. Some children with special needs may have distinctive areas of interest or talents that you can encourage. As far as possible, keep children with disabilities with their own peer group.

- If you have a child with hearing difficulties, make sure they sit near the front and that they can see the speaker's face clearly (not lit from behind). If a loop system is available, check that it is working for the child. Discussion in small groups can be hard for deaf children. Try to reduce background noise.

- Pay attention to any medical needs noted on the registration form, particularly any medication they take. Keep a record of any medication given, initialled by the first-aider and another team member.

- Designate leaders to work one-to-one with children with challenging behaviour. Where appropriate, set up a buddy system so that they work closely with a peer.

- Expect good behaviour from all children, but be tolerant of unusual behaviour. For example, some children need to fiddle with something in their hands.

- Ensure that all the children know what is planned for the day. Give the children a five minute warning when an activity is about to finish. Some children need to finish one activity before they can concentrate on another.

For more information, see *Top Tips: Welcoming special children* (SU)

WORKING WITH CHILDREN FROM OTHER FAITHS OR CULTURES

- We will not criticise, ridicule or belittle other religions.

- We will not tell the children what their faith says, nor define it by what some of its adherents do.

- We will not ask the children to say, sing or pray things that they do not believe, understand or that compromises their own faith.

- We will value and affirm the positive aspects of the children's culture.

- We will use music, artwork and methods that are culturally appropriate. For example, Asian Christian music, pictures of people from a variety of backgrounds, single sex activities where deemed appropriate.

- We will be open and honest in our presentation of the Christian faith.

- We will be open and honest about the aims and content of our work with teachers, families, carers and other adults involved in their lives.

- We will seek to build long-term friendships that are genuine and not dependent on conversion.

- Talking of conversion with children of other faiths in isolation from their families is inappropriate.

- We are committed to the long- term nature of the work, for the children now and the impact this could have on future generations.

- Where children show a genuine interest in the Christian faith we will discuss how they can be a follower of Jesus and obey their parents, whilst being open and honest about the consequences.

- We will never suggest that the children keep things secret from their families or carers.

For more information see *Top Tips: Welcoming children of other faiths* (SU)

Working with families and the community

Children are part of a family and also part of a wider network of relationships. When sharing Jesus with them, we always need to be aware of the values and backgrounds of their family. There will be repercussions on a whole family if God is making himself known to a child in that family. He may also be making himself known to family members.

Of course, we do not run a holiday club simply as a means of reaching parents and grandparents, because the children themselves matter to God. But a holiday club is an opportunity to think wider than just the children. For years, many churches have been inviting parents to come to a final event or meal or service. Parents are often glad to come, in the same way that they will attend and support a school play or assembly.

However, an outward-looking church will want to encourage family members to explore the good news of Jesus for themselves, to be active in their involvement rather than being passively appreciative. This is especially true for fathers and grandfathers who are often more comfortable to be doing things and offering their skills, than sitting around and discussing. How often has a church barbecue been run by the men in the community, gathering around the barbecue? Another example would be the men on the fringe of a church who go off for long hikes or play football or attend rugby matches together but would never go to a discussion group or even a church service. People long to be able to get involved and to recognise that they have something to contribute.

The appeal of the environment
More and more people are challenged about threats to the environment. Christians certainly don't have the monopoly of caring about the world, although they

bring to it an appreciation that this is God's good world whose protection has been entrusted to humanity. **Wastewatchers** is a very natural means of tapping into that concern.

- Why not hire a skip for the week before the club, leaflet all neighbours and invite them to deposit any of their large non-garden rubbish in it. Check with your local council that this is OK – you don't want to be encouraging fly-tipping! Suitable items can be used to build up the tip at the start of the club and anything left can be taken away. This will provide a service to the community and also encourage a lot of goodwill (and possible abuse!). It might be something the local paper would report on, providing positive advertising.

- In churches which have run environmental days/weekends, many fringe church members have helped with projects such as car washing, graffiti cleaning, bird-box making and tree planting as part of their service to the community. Often this sort of activity has led to greater involvement in the church and the building of constructive relationships.

- Running a cycling proficiency scheme or a 'human bus' that picks up children from their homes in a 'crocodile' to walk them to the club do not need to be run entirely by those who are church members (but they will need to have gone through your child protection procedure).

- Local schools might run a 'suitable' rubbish collection for the club the week before. This could be organised by a sympathetic parent. It involves people before the club even begins and is good advertising.

Above all, you should be imaginative and do what is possible!

The opportunities for extra helpers

In one regular holiday club church, there was a policy that no offer of help was refused, whether it came from church or non-church people. Of course, only those who know Jesus can talk with children about him so Taskforce Leaders need to be committed Christians, as does anyone who has a prominent up-front role. But refreshments, registration, security, craft preparation, rubbish collection, badge making or cleaning up afterwards are among tasks where fringe people can make a contribution. Explaining why it would not be suitable for them to lead a small group may provide an opportunity for explaining the spiritual aims of the club.

In one church a grandma had just become a Christian from a totally unbelieving background. She offered to help at the holiday club and was willing to do anything. The leader made sure that among the many things she did that week, she was always sitting in the main session to hear the Bible story, DVD and explanation. She was hearing all this for the first time, like most of the children, and was thrilled by what she discovered about God!

Brothers and sisters with long memories

It is amazing how often older brothers and sisters (and even parents!) who have once been part of a holiday club begin to reminisce as they pick up their siblings. It is worth considering some sort of reunion for those once involved in a club who have slipped away from anything to do with the church. This would be impossible to do if the club has not been running long or if it takes place in a highly mobile community. But in places where a club has been running for some years, it is amazing the measure of 'good feelings' that people still hold towards a church that provided them with the fun of a holiday club.
'I can still remember that Shipshapes song.'
'And do you remember the Light Factory?'
Such positive memories are a potential bridge builder! Think boldly!

Family events connected with the theme of Wastewatchers

After each session, there is a suggestion for a related additional event. Each explores the themes of **Wastewatchers**. None of them is particularly original but is a variation on what has been done many times before – but maybe not in your church! Details of each are given below. Visit the SU holiday club website bulletin board to find out what other churches have done and give advice to others: www.scriptureunion.org.uk/wastewatchers

All these suggestions require some involvement by those participating and that is quite deliberate.

Many people running a holiday club in one week have quite enough to do with just the children's programme and do not have enough leaders or energy for anything else. But in the holiday season, this daily contact with parents and carers provides opportunities for outreach that are not to be missed. Are there other people in the church who could run additional events?

Alternatively, you may wish to run events for the whole family in the weeks after the club, whether at the weekend, in an evening, in the holidays or during term-time. Building relationships and trust takes time – normally much more than what can happen in just one week. Think differently from how you have always done things. Are there other churches you could cooperate with? The suggestions below provide plenty of variety. Remember, you cannot do all of them, but resolve to explore at least one of them!

Environmental community project

In recent years, churches have engaged in projects that clean up the environment or provide services to their community. Soul Survivor has particularly played a part in encouraging this, as has been seen in Festival Manchester in 2003 and SOULINTHECITY 2004 and the NOISE projects over a number of years (check out www.soulaction.org). Projects like this have often been considered as young people's events but there is no reason why people of all ages can't get involved. It needs careful supervision, ensuring that all adults working with children are appropriately supervised. This project could run throughout the week or at the concluding weekend.

Here are some suggestions:

- Find out what local environmental groups/your local country park are doing and what help they need, or find out what national organisations are doing on a local level.
- Plant trees, flowers, shrubs in appropriate locations (maybe the local school or in OAPs' gardens)
- Make bird boxes.
- Collect cardboard or any other rubbish not collected by the local council.
- Remove graffiti.
- Grow and give away tomato plants.
- Make monkey nut strings bird feeders (in the autumn and winter).
- Encourage involvement in community trade justice issues.

> The church that trialled **Wastewatchers** organised groups of older children to make bird boxes for the local graveyard and community school. Older, often fringe, members of the church helped them. One girl who had never wielded a screwdriver before was thrilled to be having a go! This would make a very satisfying Saturday morning workshop for parents/carers and children.

Cycling proficiency

To encourage children to use their bicycles and to ride safely, explore running a cycling proficiency programme during the week for older children. Councils organise tests on a group basis through schools and youth groups. They will not teach cycling proficiency to children under

10. If you wish to organise testing, you should first contact the local school or youth group or get further advice from local council Road Safety Officers. Find out what is already happening in your area. But remember that if children come by bicycle, it is the parents' responsibility to ensure they are competent to ride and that they take responsibility for making the bicycle secure and keeping hold of helmets.

> In Lincoln a church ran a Bikewise cycling session as part of the holiday club, running the programme alongside the main group activity. Certificates were presented at the end of the week. Another year they ran a midweek session for 6 to 8 weeks. This received very positive feedback from parents.

A family banquet (Day 2)

The wedding theme of this session leads naturally onto a family banquet in the evening. Organise a special feast (without a bride or groom) where everyone dresses up smartly, wearing a button-hole or a party hat (made by the children or as a competition!). Some parents (including some who do not come to church) may offer to help prepare for this during the afternoon, along with their children. Issue special invitations, ensuring no one is excluded. You will need to decide if children can come alone if someone from their family is not with them. (A leader could take responsibility for any unaccompanied children.) Arrange for a photographer to record the event. Do not place too much stress on the wedding aspect since parents, families and children may have had mixed experiences of weddings and marriage.

After the feast, provide some entertainment, a barn dance or show the DVD episode from this session and sing a couple of songs from the club. You could also show the *Living Waterways* video on the **Wastewatchers** DVD. This will give families some idea of the theme of the week and may also inspire them to get involved with similar projects! You can also advertise the following Sunday's service and other follow-up events.

Laying on such a feast early in the programme will bring the children together, help leaders get to know the children and engage families far more.

If you wanted to be really different you could aim to make this a Fairtrade meal, making a point of only using certain Fairtrade products. Think carefully how you would explain this to children of all ages. For information on Fairtrade visit www.fairtrade.org.uk

Show a film (Day 3)

You will have spent three days discovering how Jesus came to bring about change. As a special family event, you could show the *Bible Timelife* DVD on Jesus. It is 176 minutes long, in two episodes. Do watch it beforehand to ensure you can reassure parents that it is worth seeing. You may only wish to show the first part this time. It has a PG certificate and is a powerful and gripping retelling of Jesus' life and death. Create a cinema environment with an intermission and give out popcorn or ice cream halfway through. You will have to ensure that you have received permission for any unaccompanied children to see it. A shorter retelling of Jesus' life and death is *The Miracle Maker* (U certificate).

(For details of the *Bible Timelife Jesus* DVD visit www.timelife.co.uk. For details of *The Miracle Maker* visit www.themiraclemaker.com and for permission to show it permissions@biblesociety.org.uk)

Trip to a zoo, local farm, park

During the **Wastewatchers** drama, children will have seen how a park was cleaned up and transformed. The story of A Rocha and the creation of the Minet Country Park features in *Little Green Pages*. As an afternoon or Saturday event, organise an inexpensive trip to a local outdoor location, ideally a country park or nature reserve. Of course, issues of child safety and cost abound but give this idea a second thought. Spend time together, build relationships and have fun! See below for details of a family event run by a church, which took place at Godstone Farm, Surrey.

Environmental showcase

Working with local groups, set up a variety of stalls to raise awareness of environmental and fair trade issues. For example: make bird boxes and bird food; conduct science experiments; provide information on road and home safety; taste Fairtrade food; play games to understand more about how the poor are affected by environmental and climate change; have a go at artwork using recycled or natural materials.

This could be part of an Earth Day, which includes a service, a lunch and the showcase! It takes a lot of effort but, as one church in Loughborough found out recently, it was well worth it. For help that *A Rocha* might be able to give, see page 94–95.

The RSPB run the Climate Action Award Scheme. You need to do six out of eleven activities (four if you are under 8 years old), then tell the RSPB which ones you did and you will get an award. This would be a great thing to do all together on an environmental day. For more details of how you can get hold of the free fun ideas booklet to help save the planet, visit www.rspb.org.uk

Final session (Day 5 or Sunday 2)

Some churches conclude their holiday club with a lunch or tea or barbecue for children and their families – a great opportunity to meet family members and for them to express their gratitude, which is what they usually want to do!

WE DID THIS

Godstone Farm family fun day

This is one example of what is possible. Every church needs to respond to their situation and opportunities.

Aim

• To follow up the regular work among children under 10 and their families.
• To build relationships and explore the theme of God's created world.

Setting

Godstone Farm in Surrey (www.godstonefarm.co.uk) has large open spaces/animals/adventure playground/nature walk. It is well set up for school groups with activity sheets, spinning/sheep shearing demonstrations and animal handling experiences. There is plenty to do for people of all ages for a whole day/afternoon, in family units and all together. Group discounts are available. A discount was agreed in advance, payment by attendees was made to the organiser rather than at the gate. All participants received a small discount while the rest of the money was used to buy prizes, certificates and other items.

Preparation

• A discount was negotiated and agreed with the farm.•
A field was set aside just for the group. (We were offered space to put up a marquee or the use of a barn should the weather be inclement.)
• All families were sent information about the farm and their responsibilities on the day etc.
• Families were asked to bring a packed lunch and to make a scarecrow for a competition, which would be judged by the farm manager. (We bought the prize for this from the Farm Shop.)
• We roped off an area of the field which was our base and decorated it with bunting and a big sign to say who we were.

Programme

1   Everyone assembled at the base. We talked about the programme and admired the scarecrows displayed all round our area. (This created quite a stir for other visitors to the farm!)
2   We played some get-to-know-you games. For example, tallest to shortest, oldest to youngest, eye colour groups etc. Everyone took part, including a number of grandparents and very small babies!
3   ree time when family groups (of all sizes and ombinations) explored the farm. They were asked to bring back something that made them think of God's

brilliant creation. They were asked NOT to bring back an animal or to pick/break anything living.
4   Activity sheets were given to everyone including adults. The sheet-filling was a timed exercise and we asked the children to be responsible for timing and for getting their family back to our area on time for a shared picnic lunch. A team marked the sheets and gave family team points as part of the competition for the day.
5   Lunch – this was a wonderful experience, so much chatter and sharing!
6   Potted sports in family groups. For example: dribbling a football around an obstacle course; welly wanging; egg and spoon obstacle course. We tried to have a farm theme but nothing that would exclude anyone. If one family member couldn't take part in dribbling, another stood in for them. The emphasis was on whole family participation. Points were awarded for times/accuracy.
7   Refreshments. We had ordered enough ice lollies from the shop, one for everybody. A team member collected these in cool boxes during the games. At this point, some dads decided to start a game of goal scoring. Lots of kids and dads joined in, others enjoyed their lollies.
8   Judging the scarecrow, plus prize-giving. The winning family was the first to pick their prizes out of an animal feedbag filled with sawdust. Everyone got a prize of some sort.
9   There was a time to recognise God's hand in creation in everything we'd seen that day. One family read Genesis 1, clearly, using a dramatised version of the Bible. Families brought their item (see 3 above) and placed it on a small straw bale, which was used as a focus.
10 Prayers of thanks to God for his creation, for this day, for the families we are part of and for the larger family that we had been that day. We sang songs as well, so that everyone had the chance to join in. We chose songs that would be known to as many as possible.

On another occasion we used a farmer's field for lots of barbecues. Family groups each dug a hole, filled it with charcoal and lit their barbecue. There was lots of competition over whose barbecue was the most effective – dads really competed with each other! Everyone shared their food! This was followed by a short celebration of God being with us and caring for us.

PART

5

Resources

WASTEWATCHERS DRAMA – PARK LIFE

Summary

A well-maintained but dull and lifeless park is spoiled by litter. Three teenagers help the park keeper to restore and improve it along the way by transforming the rubbish into useful things.

(Although the scripts refer to a park, the three items created – a pond, a bench and a trellis – are quite generic, so could fit into whatever you decide to transform the rubbish tip into, whether that is a nature reserve, a playground, a garden or something else.)

Characters

Harriet, Laurence and Barrington (Harry, Larry and Barry) are young people, and are best played by people in their teens. If no young people are available, adults could play these characters, but this needs to be done carefully to avoid being patronising or condescending. If in doubt, play them as adults and adapt the script accordingly. Barry is quite nasty and generally destructive, but he comes good in the end.

The park keeper is an adult. At first he goes from being proud and fastidious, to angry, to depressed. But from episode 2, he starts to learn some new attitudes to life. Confident actors, who have the time to put in the

necessary rehearsals, should play these parts. The dialogue isn't complex, but the dramas involve some slapstick routines which need practice. Actors of either sex can play the characters, if you adjust names.

Episode 1

Props: Football, feather duster, nail scissors, magnifying glass, small tin of green paint, small paintbrush, litter (including some really big stuff, even paint to create graffiti).

Sound effects: Some 'silent comedy' type chase music would be good for the chase scenes in this episode.

Scenery: A sign like this:

NO Ball Games

NO Dogs

NO Cycling

NO Skateboards

NO Picnics

NO Walking

KEEP OFF THE GRASS

You will need extras to come onto the stage to drop their litter.

Summary: A perfect lawn – the park keeper's pride and joy – is spoiled by litter.

Script

Harry, Larry and Barry enter. Larry is bouncing a football.

Larry: I bet I'll score more goals than you.

Barry: Oh no you won't.

Larry: Oh yes I will.

Barry: I'm the best footballer in the country!

Larry: Well I'm the best footballer in the world!

Barry: I'm the best footballer in the galaxy!

Larry: I'm the best footballer in the whole universe!

Harry: Well I bet neither of you scores any goals. Look.

(They look at the sign.)

Larry: No ball games?

Barry: What sort of a park is that?

Harry: A rubbish park! Come on, let's go and do something else. *(All three leave.)*

(The park keeper enters, tuts, and then uses a feather duster to remove a speck of dust from the lawn. Only then does he notice the children.)

Park keeper: Oh, hello. I didn't see you there. I expect you were admiring my magnificent lawn. I hope none of you trod on it! It takes me hours to get it looking this good. Oh. Hold on a minute. There's a bit sticking up there. *(He takes out a pair of nail scissors and a magnifying glass, and moves as if to step on the grass.)* Oops! Nearly forgot! *(He takes off his shoes and socks, then steps very carefully onto the grass, before trimming an imaginary blade with the nail scissors.)* That's better! Oh no, hang on a minute. *(He takes out a tin of green paint, and a very fine paintbrush, which he uses to touch up another blade of grass.)* That one was going a little bit brown! *(He holds up his fingers, which have paint on them.)* I don't like to boast, but I'm a pretty good park keeper. Everyone says I've got green fingers! In fact, I've invented my very own special lawn food. I've been making it in the shed. In fact, it should be ready by now. Would you do me a favour while I go and fetch it? I'm worried that while I'm away, someone might walk on my lawn. So if you see anyone step on my grass, could you shout, 'Parky, there's malarkey!' as loud as you can? Great. Let's have a practice. Ready? *(He lifts up his foot as if to step on the lawn. Other leaders should lead the children in shouting, 'Parky, there's malarkey!')* That's brilliant. I know the park will be in safe hands with you guarding it. Back in a minute. *(He exits.)*

(A couple of the extras walk onto the stage, eating crisps and carrying newspapers etc. Prompted by the other leaders if necessary, the children shout, 'Parky, there's malarkey!' The park keeper returns, and walks to the front of the stage, facing the children.)

Park keeper : Malarkey? Where?

Children and leaders: Behind you!

(The park keeper turns around, but the others move so that they are still behind him. The park keeper asks the children again and again. Eventually, the park keeper spots the others and chases them, which causes them to drop their packets, papers etc before they run away.)

Park keeper: Thanks for guarding the park. Let me know if anyone else comes, won't you? Thanks. *(He exits in pursuit of the others.)*

(Two more extras enter with more rubbish. The children should shout but the park keeper doesn't appear. 'Extra 1' drops litter.)

Extra 2: Hey! You shouldn't drop litter!

Extra 1: It doesn't matter. Look, there's already rubbish on the ground.

Extra 2: So what?

Extra 1: So, someone's going to have to clear up anyway. If there's already litter, it doesn't matter if we drop some.

Extra 2: *(To the children.)* Do you think that's right? Do you think we should pick it up? *(The children should respond by shouting, 'Yes')*

Extra 1: You see? They're shouting, 'Yes'. They think what I said was right!

Extra 2: *(To the children.)* Really? Oh well, if you're sure… *(They both empty all the rubbish from their pockets and bags.)*

(They exit and the park keeper returns.)

Park keeper: What a mess! Why didn't you tell me that someone was here? *(The children should protest that they did.)*

Park keeper: Oh no you didn't!

Children and leaders: Oh yes we did!

(This is repeated a few times.)

Park keeper: Well, I'm going to go and get a rubbish bag. Don't bother to shout. I won't be able to hear you anyway.

(The park keeper exits. While he is absent, various extras enter with big rubbish (old bike, box of tin cans etc). They look around furtively, then dump it and exit. If possible add some graffiti to the background.)

(Harry, Barry and Larry return.)

Harry: Gosh! What a mess!

Barry: How did that happen so quickly?

(The park keeper returns.)

Park keeper: Oi! You three! What have you done to my park?

Larry: It wasn't us!

Park keeper: Don't lie. I know what you kids are like! Come here! *(He chases them off the stage. All the time they are protesting their innocence.)*

Episode 2

Props: Football, feather duster, something to be the pond – preferably a bath, but could be a basin or a bowl inside a tyre if space or resources are limited.

Scenery: Much more rubbish has arrived since yesterday.

Summary: Harry, Larry and Barry return. The park keeper is depressed. They explain that they didn't make the mess and try to cheer him up. Then they offer to help him to clear up the mess, but they realise that they can't possibly shift all the rubbish. So they decide to use it instead to create something constructive. They decide to create a pond from an old bath, and go to get some spades.

Script

Much more rubbish has arrived since yesterday. The park keeper is sitting despondently in the middle of it all. Harry, Larry and Barry enter from the back, and walk through the children to the stage area. They don't notice the state of the park until the appropriate moment. Barry is carrying a football.

Larry: I hope the park's all right now. We'll never be able to play football if it's still full of rubbish.

Barry: Oh, I don't know Larry – you support [insert name of local team], so you should be used to rubbish football!

Harry: Don't worry. You saw that park keeper. He's bound to have tidied it all up by now.

Larry: Yes, but if he has, he won't let us play football on it anyway. You know what he's like.

Harry: I've thought of that! We'll be okay, because he'll be too busy chasing the people who made the mess to worry about us.

Barry: *(Sincerely.)* Oh yeah! Brilliant! You're a genius you are Harry!

Harry: Thanks, Barry. What do you think, Larry?

Larry: I think your plan is just like the park keeper's park.

Harry: *(Smugly.)* You mean it's really neat and perfect?

Larry: No. I mean it's a load of rubbish! Look. *(They look, and see that the park is now worse than ever.)*

Barry: Hey – there's the park keeper. *(He starts chanting loudly.)* What a load of rubbish! What a load of rubbish!

Larry: Sssssh!

Park keeper: Oh. It's you lot. Hooligans!

Harry: What do you mean?

Larry: *(To Harry.)* That's what I was trying to tell you. The park keeper thinks it was us that ruined his park. That's why your plan was rubbish!

Park keeper: *(Sadly.)* Why are you picking on me? Isn't it enough that you've ruined my park?

Barry: *(Ignoring him and chanting.)* What a load of OUCH! *(Harry has kicked him. He starts to hop about, holding his shin.)*

Harry: Barrington!

Larry: 'Barrington'?! I often wondered what Barry was short for… *(He collapses, laughing.)*

Harry: *(To park keeper.)* It wasn't us! In fact, we've come to cheer you up!

Park keeper: Really?

Harry: Yes. Barry's going to tell you a joke.

Barry: I am?

Harry: Yes, you are.

Barry: OK, er… Knock, knock!

Park keeper: Who's there?

Barry: Lydia

Park keeper: Lydia who?

Barry: Lydia dustbin has just fallen off!

Park keeper: Dustbin? Boo-hoo-hoo! *(He bursts into tears.)*

Harry: *(Annoyed, to Barry.)* That was a rubbish joke.

Park keeper: Rubbish? Boo-hoo-hoo!

Harry: OK. Try to think of something nice.

Barry: Yes, that's a good tip.

Park keeper: Tip? Boo-hoo-hoo!

Larry: There must be something that would cheer you up.

Park keeper: Well, sometimes it cheers me up when I think about my dog, Trudy.

Larry: Great. Think about Trudy, then. Better still; imagine lots of dogs just like Trudy. Imagine Trudy with a whole litter of puppies!

Park keeper: Litter? Boo-hoo-hoo!

Larry: *(To Harry.)* It's not working!

Harry: There must be something that will cheer him up. I refuse to give up!

Park keeper: Refuse? Boo-hoo-hoo!

Larry: Please don't cry. Look, we'll help you to clear it all up!

Barry: Oh no we won't!

Larry and Harry: *(Encouraging the children to join in.)* Oh yes we will!

Barry: Oh no we won't!

Larry and Harry and children: Oh yes we will!

(Repeat a few times.)

Harry: *(Picking up some rubbish.)* Barry, you tidy up a bit. Larry, hold this.

Barry: *(Picking up the park keeper's feather duster.)* This should come in useful.

(Harry and the park keeper pick up various things and place them in Larry's arms, until Larry is overburdened and struggles to hold everything. Meanwhile, Barry is dusting various things. The actors should ad lib during this part.)

Barry: *(Looking at Larry.)* Gosh, look at the dust on this! *(He starts to dust Larry with the feather duster.)*

Larry: Hey! Get off! That tickles! *(Larry starts to squirm and giggle, but Barry carries on, until Larry eventually drops everything he's holding.)*

Park keeper: It's no use. We'll never be able to clear all this stuff.

Larry: *(Has a flash of inspiration.)* Maybe we don't have to.

Barry: Oh good! Let's go home then. Bye! *(He starts to walk off.)*

Larry: No wait! Bring me that bath [or basin, bowl, or whatever you're using].

Barry: I've already dusted you. Surely you don't need a bath as well?

Larry: No. Look. We can put it into the ground, and then it'll be a —

Barry: Mud bath!

Larry: Pond. We can turn this old bath into a beautiful pond.

Barry: *(Sarcastically.)* Oh yeah, great idea! Who's going to want to come and see a pond in the middle of a rubbish tip?

Larry: It won't be a rubbish tip, because we're going to do the same thing with all the other rubbish.

Park keeper: What – bury it?

Larry: No, turn it into something useful. If we can't transport it to somewhere else, we can transform it into something else.

Harry: Like what?

Larry: Oh, I don't know. There must be loads of exciting things we can do with all this stuff.

Barry: I know! We could make a pond from this old bath.

Larry: *(Sarcastically.)* Brilliant! Why didn't I think of that?

Harry: *(To park keeper.)* Do you have any shovels we could use?

Park keeper: Yes. They're in the shed.

Larry: Come on then, let's go and fetch them. *(They start to exit.)*

Barry: Hey – what do you call a man with a spade on his head?

Harry: I don't know, what do you call a man with a spade on his head?

Barry: Doug! *(The others groan.)* And what do you call a man without a spade on his head?

Larry: I don't know, what do you call a man without a spade on his head?

Barry: Douglas! *(The others groan even more. They all exit.)*

Harry: *(Off stage.)* Barrington!

Episode 3

Props: Three blindfolds, a large box, at least one chair, some (water-based) white paint and a brush. Barry should wear old clothes.

Sound effects: Slapstick noises, a heavy object falling.

Scenery: The pond and the area around it has been tidied up since Episode 2, and some of the other rubbish has been cleared.

Summary: The park keeper leads in the other three, who are all blindfolded because he wants to surprise them with the finished pond. Barry decides to keep his blindfold on so that he can't do any work. Because he is blindfolded, Barry gets in the way and is almost squashed by a big box. Harry paints an old chair to make a bench, and Barry, who is still blindfolded, sits in the wet paint.

Script

The park keeper leads in the other three, who are all blindfolded.

Barry: Are we nearly there yet?

Park keeper: Not far now.

Harry: Why do we have to be blindfolded?

Park keeper: I want it to be a surprise.

Larry: What?

Park keeper: If I tell you, it won't be a surprise, will it?

Larry: Oh yeah! I see.

Barry: I don't. I can't see a thing.

(They walk on. Suddenly, Larry stops, and all the others collide with him.)

Harry: What did you stop for?

Larry: I think I've just trodden in something. Eugh!

Park keeper: Here we are. You can look now.

(They remove their blindfolds.)

Harry: Wow! You've totally transformed that pond!

Barry: Bath, you mean.

Larry: It was a bath, but now it's a pond. It's fantastic!

Harry: You must have worked all night.

Park keeper: Well, I was up quite late. But I had to stop when it got dark. You can't really work when you can't see what you're doing.

Barry: *(Putting on his blindfold.)* Oh dear – I can't see now. That means I can't do any work. What a shame!

Larry: Just ignore him. What do we need to do today?

Park keeper: Well, it's still a bit dark and gloomy. I think we need to make it lighter.

Harry: How can we do that?

Barry: Set fire to it! That'll make lots of light!

Larry: Barrington! *(To park keeper.)* Just ignore him. We could start by clearing some of this rubbish to let more light in.

Harry: And there are some old paint tins over there. Maybe we can paint some old chairs white, to make a nice bright park bench.

Park keeper: Good idea! Harry, you paint the chairs. Larry, come and help me with this box.

(Harry displays a 'wet paint' sign, and begins to paint an old chair.)

Larry: OK. *(They hold each end of a box that is situated behind Barry.)*

Barry: I'll just sit here, then, until you've finished.

Park keeper: Ready… Lift! *(They lift the box up and backwards. At the same time, Barry sits down where he expects the box to be and falls on the floor. A 'clown' sound effect is heard.)*

Barry: Ouch! *(Barry is now lying on the floor, directly underneath the large box the other two are holding.)*

Larry: This is really heavy. I can't hold it much longer!

Harry: Barry! Get up!

Barry: Sorry, I can't do any work today. I think I'll just lie here and have a sleep.

Larry: I think I'm going to drop it!

Harry: Barry! You're in danger! *(Harry tries to pull him out of the way by his legs.)*

Barry: I don't believe you. You're just pulling my leg.

Larry: I can't… hold it… any… more! *(On the word, 'more', the park keeper and Larry drop the box – use a suitable sound effect to give the impression that it is very heavy. At the same instant, Harry pulls Barry out of the way by pulling his legs.)*

Barry: Hey! Now you're really pulling my leg. Get off!

Park keeper: Barry, It's about time you started pulling your weight around here!

Barry: I don't need to – Harry's pulling my weight at the moment!

Harry: *(Finally letting go of his leg.)* Barrington, I'm getting cross with you now. Take that blindfold off and help! *(Barry, still blindfolded, walks towards the painted chair.)*

Barry: I'd love to help, but my leg hurts, thanks to you! I just need to sit down.

Park keeper: I don't think you should sit down there, Barry.

Barry: Just stop being so bossy and let me sit down for a moment.

Park keeper: *(To the children.)* Do you think we should let him sit down?

Barry: *(Encouraging the children to join in.)* Yes!

Park keeper: Are you sure?

Barry and children: Yes!

Park keeper: *(To Barry.)* Do you think I should let you?

Barry: Definitely!

Park keeper: OK then. You asked for it. Sit! *(Barry sits.)*

Barry: Ah! That's better.

Harry: Yes, you'll be all white now! *(Said as if saying 'all right now'.)*

Larry: Now, do you think you could help us?

Barry: OK. *(He tries to get up, but is stuck to the chair. He makes a big effort and manages to get to his feet, but is still stuck to the chair. He walks around for a bit like this. Then he manages to free himself from the chair, and turns his back to the children to reveal the white paint all over his back and bottom. The others laugh.)* What are you laughing at?

Larry: If you take your blindfold off, you'll see.

Barry: *(He removes his blindfold.)* Where's the joke then?

All: It's behind you!

Barry: *(Turning around to look behind.)* There's nothing there! Where is it?

All: It's behind you!

Barry: *(Turning around to face the front again.)* Oh no it isn't!

All: *(Encouraging the children to join in.)* Oh yes it is!

Barry: Oh no it isn't!

All: Oh yes it is!

(Repeat a few times, until Barry looks at his back.)

Barry: Oh no! My mum'll kill me!

Park keeper: Don't worry Barry, I've got something that'll clean it off. Come on Harry; we'd better wash the paint off your hands, too.

(The park keeper and Barry exit, Larry goes with them.)

Harry: Well, that was a busy day. I think I need a sit down after all that excitement. *(She goes as if to sit down on the painted chair, but just before her bottom touches it she stops and stands up again.)* Had you going there, didn't I? See you all tomorrow. Bye!

(Harry exits.)

Episode 4

Props: Picnic basket or coolbox. The sign from Episode 1.

Scenery: There is now a white bench, which incorporates the chair from Episode 3 (eg two chairs with a plank laid across the seats). The area around the bench should also be tidy. There is a pile of branches on one side of the stage. In the pile should be at least two long branches or planks.

Summary: They decide to build a trellis from some long branches, but Barry keeps narrowly missing* Larry's head with a branch. When Larry bumps his head he becomes cross with Barry and walks off, followed by Harry. Barry and the park keeper then have a heart to heart, and they both realise that they need to change.

*The script says that Larry should duck so that the branch misses his head. But for better comic effect, the branch should appear to hit him each time. This requires that the branch being swung round is stopped a fraction before it hits him. However, this variation should not be attempted unless it is very carefully rehearsed and choreographed!

Script

The park keeper leads in the other three. He is carrying a basket. They enter from the back and walk through the group of children.

Larry: Oh no! What's happened to the grass? It looks dead!

Barry: *(Looking at the children.)* And it's full of worms, and slugs. Urgh!

Harry: *(Also looking at the children.)* And there are loads of weeds too! Looks like your special lawn food recipe was a bit of a dead loss!

Park keeper: Don't worry. That's the way the lawn food works. It kills off the lawn to make it grow stronger. Tomorrow, it will be more full of life than ever before – you'll see.

Larry: What have you got in the basket?

Park keeper: Well, I thought we might have a little snack before we start.

Harry: Great! We can sit on the new bench.

Barry: No way! I'm not falling for that again!

Larry: It's OK, Barry. The paint's dry now.

Barry: *(Cynically.)* Yeah, right. You sit on the bench if you like. I'm going to sit over there.

Park keeper: OK. Suit yourself. *(He sits on the bench with Harry and Larry.)*

Larry: You've done a good job on this bench, Harry.

Barry: Huh! This pile of old branches looks much more comfortable. *(He sits down, but leaps up again immediately, clutching his bottom.)* Ouch!

Harry: What's the matter?

Barry: This pile of branches is full of thorns!

Larry: *(Going over to have a look.)* Oh yeah! There are some stinging nettles too.

Barry: Where?

Larry: *(Poking his finger into the pile.)* Just there. Ouch! *(He sucks his finger.)*

Park keeper: I think that stuff's a bit dangerous. Perhaps we'd better clear all the dead wood and leaves before we have a snack.

Barry: Hey, what do you call a man with a pile of leaves on his head?

Harry: I don't know, what do you call a man with a pile of leaves on his head?

Barry: Russell!

Larry: That's terrible!

Barry: You don't think I should branch out into comedy then?

Harry: No, leave the jokes to the experts.

Park keeper: You're hardly a budding comedian!

Larry: Yes, I think you should stick to helping us.

Harry: You can start by helping with these branches.

Barry: Are we going to burn them? Great!

Park keeper: No, we're not going to burn them. We're going to make a trellis.

Barry: A what?

Harry: A trellis. It's a kind of archway for plants to grow up.

Barry: How can we make a trellis from this old junk?

Park keeper: Find me some nice long bits of wood and I'll show you.

Larry: OK. Come on Barry.

(They go over to the pile of branches. Larry needs to be further from the other characters than Barry.)

Barry: Here's a good one. *(He picks it up and puts it on his shoulder.)* What d'you think Larry? *(He turns around, so that the branch narrowly misses Larry's head, causing him to duck.)*

Harry: Careful, Barry!

Barry: Why? *(As he says this, he turns the other way, thus narrowly missing Larry with the other end of the branch.)*

Larry: You nearly hit me! *(Barry turns towards Larry. Larry has to duck again.)*

Park keeper: Stop doing that.

Barry: What? *(Barry turns, Larry ducks again. Larry sits down.)*

Harry: Just stand still. Don't move a muscle.

Park keeper: Are you OK, Larry?

Larry: Yes, I think so. *(He stands up, and bangs his head on the branch that Barry is still holding.)* Ouch!

Harry: Careful!

Barry: Yes, be careful – you might have broken my branch!

Larry: *(Crossly.)* That's it! I've had enough! You're always causing trouble Barry. I'm not working with you any more. Goodbye! *(He exits.)*

Barry: What's the matter with him? He's like a bear with a sore head!

Harry: That's typical of your attitude, Barry. You don't care about anything or anyone apart from yourself! I'm going to go and see if Larry's okay. *(She exits in the same direction as Larry.)*

Barry: What's her problem? She's talking nonsense!

Park keeper: Oh no she isn't

Barry: Oh yes she is.

Park keeper: *(Encouraging the children to join in.)* Oh no she isn't.

Barry: Oh yes she is.

Park keeper and children: Oh no she isn't!

(This carries on for a while.)

Barry: But I was only trying to help! It wasn't my fault that Larry banged his head! *(He throws the branch down in disgust.)*

Park keeper: Maybe not, but you can see their point, can't you?

Barry: What do you mean?

Park keeper: Well, you haven't been all that helpful these past few days. You've just wanted to mess around, or do nothing and watch everybody else work. Don't you care about the park, Barry?

Barry: Yes I do! But what's the point of making the park nice again if nobody is allowed to enjoy it?

Park keeper: What do you mean?

Barry: *(Picking up the sign from Episode 1.)* You seem to care more about the park than about people. How can anybody enjoy the park with all these rules? At least if it's a rubbish tip we'll be able to play in it!

Park keeper: *(Slowly, as if realising it for the first time.)* You know – I never realised that people felt like that! I thought my park was perfect, but actually it was rubbish, because nobody could enjoy it. I guess I've been a bit selfish.

Barry: I think we both have.

Park keeper: I'll tell you what; if I promise not to put these rules back up, will you help me to make the park beautiful again so that everyone can enjoy it?

Barry: That's a deal!

Park keeper: Great! *(He picks up two long branches, and holds them upright, one in each hand, with their ends* *resting on the floor.)* Now, if I hold these steady, can you tie a piece across the top?

Barry: Sorry, I can't help right this minute.

Park keeper: But you promised!

Barry: I know, but there's something I've got to do first. I need to go and make up with Harry and Larry. I'll be back soon! *(He exits.)*

Park keeper: OK. I'd better get the top piece myself then. *(He lets go of the upright branches in order to go and fetch the top piece. But as he does so, they begin to fall over, so he dashes back to catch them. Repeat this a few times.)* Oh dear, I think I'm going to need some help! He lays the branches on the floor. Barry! Wait for me! *(He exits in the same direction as Barry.)*

Episode 5

Props: Signs saying 'Litter', 'Brown', 'Green' and 'Clear'; the 'Wet Paint' sign from Episode 3; the large sign from Episode 1; a barrel (or something else to use for a litter bin); three large boxes – the boxes will become the bottle bank, so should ideally be fairly plain (perhaps painted green, brown and white). It would be a good idea to pre-cut the holes in them, leaving only the corners attached, so that the holes can be made quickly at the appropriate point in the script. Initially, these boxes are filled with junk that can be used for musical instruments. For example:

For the cast: glass bottles filled with water to different levels, and something to hit them with; hose pipe/watering can etc that can be blown like a trumpet (insert a proper trumpet mouthpiece to make this easier). For the children: tin can/saucepan/plastic container drums; saucepan lid cymbals; shakers made from plastic bottles filled with gravel; cellophane to make a scrunching noise; claves made from old bits of wood; a 'bumpy' squash bottle to rub a stick against; bits of sandpaper to rub together (all these items must be safe and free of sharp edges and splinters). The children may have made instruments as a craft activity.

Sound effects: If possible, play some birdsong throughout this episode, to reinforce the idea of the park being full of life. Suitable music for the celebration.

Scenery: The trellis is now finished. There is more life in evidence in the park – colourful flowers, plants on the trellis, ducks in the pond etc. There is a barrel and three boxes of 'junk' as described above.

Summary: The park is now finished. It is full of life and much more attractive, apart from the items listed in 'scenery' above. The characters create a litter bin and a bottle bank, to make sure that the park will stay tidy. They change the sign from Episode 1, by deleting all the 'NO's and writing 'All welcome' in place of 'Keep off the grass'. Then they celebrate by making music from rubbish!

Script

The characters enter together from the back and walk through the group of children.

Larry: Wow! *(Looking at the children.)* Your special lawn food really does work! This grassy area looks great!

Barry: And look at the trellis! We only finished it last night, but it's covered in plants already!

Park keeper: Well, I put a bit of lawn food on that, too.

Larry: There are even ducks in the pond! Don't tell me your lawn food made the ducks grow too!

Park keeper: Of course not. That would be quackers!

Barry: I didn't know ducks liked crackers.

Larry: I don't know about crackers, but they certainly like bread.

Barry: What's bread got to do with it?

Harry: Oh use your loaf, Barry. We left our picnic here yesterday, and the ducks must have been attracted by the bread!

Barry: Crumbs!

Harry: Ooh, look at those beautiful flowers! Are you going to pick some for me Larry?

Larry: *(Emphatically.)* No I'm not!

Harry: Oh. Don't you love me Larry? Go on, give us a kiss! *(She chases Larry.)*

Larry: All right, all right! I'll pick you some flowers if you promise to stop trying to kiss me!

Park keeper: No, Larry. You mustn't pick the flowers. We have to leave them there for everyone else to enjoy.

Barry: But what about what you said yesterday? You promised that you'd let people enjoy the park and not have lots of silly rules.

Park keeper: Yes I did, but that doesn't mean that people can do what they like.

Harry: He's right. We can enjoy the park, but we have to look after it so that everyone else can enjoy it too. I'm sorry I asked you to pick the flowers, Larry.

Larry: That's OK.

Harry: Do you forgive me?

Larry: Of course.

Harry: Give us a kiss, then! *(She moves towards Larry, who backs away.)*

Park keeper: There's no time for that, I need you to help me put these signs up!

Barry: Signs? But you promised that you wouldn't put the rules back up.

Park keeper: These are different signs. Look, this one says, 'Litter'.

Larry: I don't understand. You're not going to put up a sign telling people to drop litter?

Park keeper: Oh yes I am!

Harry: But that's silly!

Park keeper: That depends where you put it. Barry, go and fetch that barrel [or box etc] over there. *(Barry fetches* *it and the park keeper attaches the sign to it.)* There. That should help to keep the park tidy.

Larry: Oh, I see! What other signs have you got?

Park keeper: *(Giving each of them a sign.)* Here you are. There's one each.

Harry: *(Holding up her sign.)* This says, 'Green'. That plant is green, so I suppose I should stick it on that. What a brilliant idea, to help colour blind people enjoy the park too.

Larry: And this one says, 'Brown', so I'll stick it onto this brown tree trunk.

Harry: What does yours say Barry? Blue? Yellow?

Barry: No. Mine says, 'Clear'. But the only clear thing here is the water in the pond, and I can't stick it onto that!

Park keeper: Go and fetch those three boxes for me, please. *(They each collect one box. They tip out the contents and bring the empty boxes to the park keeper.)* Now, I need to make a hole in each one, while you go and fetch your signs, please… And we'll stick your signs above each of the holes.

Larry: Oh, I see! It's a bottle bank!

Harry: Brilliant! People can recycle their bottles instead of just throwing them away!

Park keeper: Now, there's just one more sign to put up. *(He holds up the sign from Episode 1.)*

Barry: But you promised!

Park keeper: Trust me, Barry. *(He puts the sign up.)* Now, Harry, have you still got some paint left from that bench?

Harry: Yes. Here it is.

Park keeper: Thanks. *(He paints over all the 'NO's and 'Keep off the grass'. Then writes 'All welcome' at the bottom, so that the sign now reads, 'Ball games, Dogs, Cycling, Skateboards, Picnics, Walking – All welcome'.)* That's better!

Barry: Actually, I think there's one more sign needed.

Larry: What's that?

Barry: This one! *(He produces the 'Wet Paint' sign.)*

Park keeper: Good thinking, Barry. I now declare this park officially open!

Harry: Hold on a minute, what about all that junk over there?

Park keeper: That's not junk. That's musical instruments for the opening celebration. Perhaps you could help me give them out. *(They all give out the 'instruments' to the children.)* Ready? Let's celebrate!

(Play some suitable music, and involve the children in singing and dancing. The idea is that the drama today doesn't have a definite ending; instead, the celebratory atmosphere flows seamlessly into some singing at the end of the session.)

BIBLE DISCOVERY NOTES FOR TASKFORCE LEADERS

The Bible discovery time is the opportunity for leaders and children to read God's Word together. Children can explore their relationship with God and can also see in practice how much Jesus matters to their leaders. The notes on the following two pages will help Taskforce Leaders talk naturally with the children. *Little Green Pages* provides additional material for older children. If you are not using it, adapt the puzzles and ideas included in the Eco Sheet after each session. These are for younger children and are photocopiable. Photocopy the Bible discovery notes and give to Taskforce Leaders.

Day 1: From nothing to something

Aim: To marvel at God's beautiful world; to recognise that things have gone wrong and how we are a part of that.

Bible passage: Genesis 1:20–27,27–31

Older children: *Little Green Pages* **pages 6-12**
Each child chooses their favourite animal/bird from the categories in the list in Genesis 1:20–27. Why did they choose that? Share your favourite animal. Read verse 25 again. Do the puzzles on pages 10 and 12 and read Genesis 1:27–31. If time, explore Genesis 3.

Younger children
Read out loud Genesis 1:20–27 asking children to listen out for their favourite type of animal. Do the Eco Sheet.

Pray together
Ask each child in turn to say the following words, filling in the name of their favourite animal/bird etc: 'Thank you God that you made _____.' After each child has spoken, everyone says together, 'God saw that everything was very good.'

Talk about
As you do the puzzles, talk about the wonder of the world God has made. God had planned for it to be orderly and beautiful. There were no mistakes. Share your enthusiasms. Ask them what things are wrong in the world. Share with them that God never intended this to happen. Ask them the reasons in the story why things went wrong. What did God want people to do in the world? Talk about what you are going to do for your community.

Day 2: From water to wine

Aim: To explore how Jesus came into the world to help people when things go wrong; to see that Jesus is with us all the time to help us.

Bible passage: John 2:1–11

Older children: *Little Green Pages* **pages 20–23**
First, write in a speech bubble what Mary, Jesus and the man in charge of the feast say. (Only include the last few words of the man in charge in verse 10.) Give these bubbles out to be held up when the Bible is read out. Read John 2:1–11 as a play with Mary, Jesus, the man in charge of the feast and a confident reader as narrator. Explore the story adapting the questions below. Do the puzzles on pages 22–23.

Younger children
Read out loud from the Bible this story from John 2:1–11 before you have refreshments. Give out empty cups. Only fill them after you have explored the story and helped them to understand what an amazing thing Jesus had done! Complete the Eco Sheet.

Pray together
Identify something each child finds difficult. Ask Jesus to help each child just as he helped at the wedding. Encourage children to talk to Jesus themselves.

Talk about
- What can go wrong at a wedding? (Give examples.) How disappointed would you be if there were no refreshments today?
- How would you have felt if you were the groom at this wedding? Talk about feeling embarrassed and what the children's experience is of that.
- What sort of things does your mum ask you to do? Why do you think Mary asked Jesus to do something?
- How would you have felt, if you were the groom, when you realised what Jesus had done?
- What might Mary and the disciples be thinking about Jesus as they walked home at the end of the day?
- Give personal experience of how Jesus helped you when you had a problem.

Day 3: From darkness into light

Aim: To hear how the blind man could see and put his trust in Jesus; to explore how the Pharisees were in darkness and needed Jesus' light to shine onto them. We too need his light to show us both the dark in our lives and also to be light like Jesus.

Bible passage: John 9:1–41

Older children: *Little Green Pages* **pages 30–34**
Provide enough copies of John 9:1–41 for each child; some brown-coloured flour and water paste and a blown-up balloon with a face drawn on – leave the eyes without irises. As the children read out the story (this could be done in a narrative way), put the brown paste on the eyes on the balloon face and then wash it off! Draw in the irises and eyelashes to make the eyes more seeing. Look up the following verses and write down what people said about Jesus from verses 16, 17, 23 and 24. If you are not using the booklet, divide a page into two columns, labelled 'What the Pharisees said' and 'What the man said'. Answer the question 'What did Jesus say about himself?' using verses 5 and 39.

Younger children
Read out loud the story using the mud as above. Talk about imagining what it is like not to be unable to see. Do the Eco Sheet together.

Pray together
Identify something all children think is bad or dark and/or a situation where they want to see Jesus shining his light. Then ask Jesus to do that. Use the teardrop and light bulb idea on the Eco Sheet. 'We thank you Jesus that you are the light for the world. We pray that you will

shine your light in _____ (ask the children to speak out their 'places'). We pray too that you will shine your light in us. Amen.'

Talk about
- Imagine what it is like to be blind. Explore the reasons why people cannot see.
- Was this man blind because he had done wrong or his parents had done wrong or neither?
- Why weren't the Pharisees really glad that this blind man could now see? Why do you think people did not like someone like Jesus who was so good and kind?
- How did Jesus show his care for the man?
- The Pharisees or teachers of the law could all see, but Jesus said they were blind. What did he mean? (The Pharisees were so busy keeping the Law that they were blinded to the truth of who Jesus was.)
- What does it mean to be blind or dark inside? (Talk about what it means to have Jesus' light inside you and to know that Jesus is with you.)

Day 4: From death to life

Aim: To hear the story of Jesus' death and discover it was part of God's plan. Jesus' death makes it possible for God to forgive us for the wrong we have done. Jesus came to take the blame for all the wrong things we have done, even though he did not deserve to die. (You will want to explain something about Jesus' coming alive.)

Bible passage: John 19:25–30; (if time) 20:1–10

Older children: *Little Green Pages* pages 38–39
Enough copies of John 19:25–30 for each child. Ask the children to underline all the words Jesus said when he was on the cross. Refer to 20:1–10 to explain the resurrection. Explore the story adapting the questions below. Do the puzzle on page 39.

Younger children
Read out loud John 19: 25–27 (miss out the names of the other women) and then 28–30. Remind children that this is very sad but it was not the end because Jesus came alive again. Then complete the Eco Sheet.

Pray together
Encourage children to think about wrong things in the world and/or in their own lives.
Thank Jesus that his death was not an accident but that he had to die to put wrong things right. If any child wants to know more about what his death means for them or for this world, make time to talk with them.

Talk about
- Even though Jesus was in awful pain, how did he go on showing his love for other people?
- What do you think Jesus meant when he said,

'Everything is done!'?
- What had Jesus come to do? Turn back to pages 24–25 and read John 3:13–15. Ask the children what they remember about the story of the bronze snake. Ask them to put a sparkle around the word 'light' and a dark cloud around the word 'dark' or 'evil' in verses 19–21.
- Remind the children of the *Learn and remember* verse and see if they can remember yesterday's story: Jesus has come to shine his light to show where there is darkness and sin; Jesus came to shine his light that gives life, which was what he gave the blind man.
- Talk about what Jesus' death means to you, why he died and why it is important that he came alive again.

Day 5: From sadness to joy

Aim: To explore the story of Jesus' meeting with Mary three days after his death; to discover that Jesus is alive today and wants to have a lifelong relationship with us.

Bible passage: John 20:11–18

Older children: *Little Green Pages* pages 40–42
Enough copies of John 20:11–18 for each child and at least three teardrops to be made into faces for each child. (If you read from verse 1, you will need more than three teardrops!) As you read the story, let the children fill in their faces. Do the puzzle on page 42.

Younger children
Give out today's Eco Sheet. Tell the children to fill in Mary's two facial expressions. Read John 20:11-18 so they can do that. Complete the Eco Sheet.

Pray together
Invite each child to finish this prayer. 'Thank you Jesus that you are alive. Thank you that you are with me (in the playground, in bed etc).' Pass round an object such as a cross. Only the child who holds this object speaks.

Talk about
- When have the children have been really sad? Share your own sad experience.
- What stopped them/you being sad?
- What stopped Mary being sad? How does knowing Jesus stop you being sad?
- If Jesus is still alive and with us, by his Spirit, as was explained earlier, what does that mean for the children in practical ways? (He is with them in the playground, when they are scared, happy, moving to a new school)
- If appropriate talk about how we can become a friend of Jesus, using an appropriately aged commitment booklet (see inside front cover)

WASTEWATCHERS REGISTRATION FORM *(Please use a separate form for each child.)*

Wastewatchers will take place at

from   to   . Please fill in this form to book a place for your child.

Child's full name	Sex: **M / F**

Date of birth	School

Please register my child for Wastewatchers	Parent's/Guardian's signature

Parent's/Guardian's full name

Address

Phone number

I give permission for my child's and my details to be entered on the church database.   **Yes / No**

WASTEWATCHERS CONSENT FORM *(Please use a separate form for each child.)*

Child's full name	

Address	

Emergency contact name	Phone number

GP's name	GP's phone number

Any known allergies or conditions

I confirm that the above details are complete and correct to the best of my knowledge.

In the unlikely event of illness or accident, I give permission for any appropriate first aid to be given by the nominated first-aider. In an emergency, and if I cannot be contacted, I am willing for my child to be given hospital treatment, including anaesthetic if necessary. I understand that every effort will be made to contact me as soon as possible.

Signature of parent/guardian: Date:

PARENT/GUARDIAN
COLLECTION SLIP

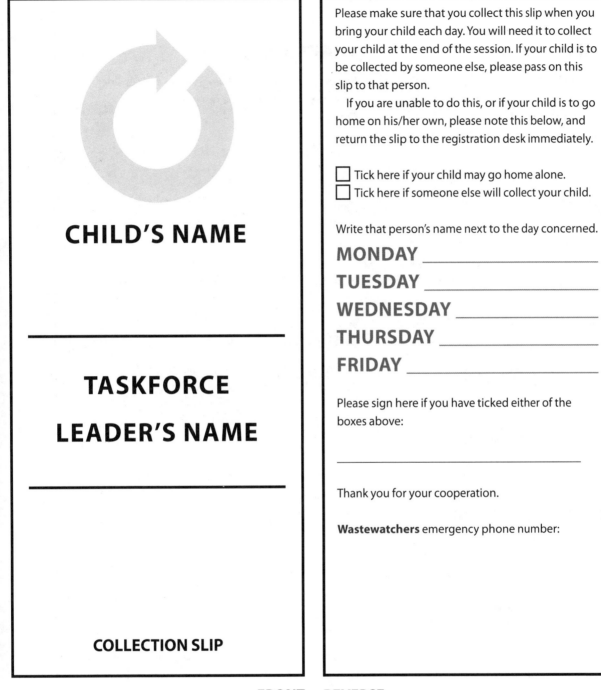

CHILD'S NAME

_____

TASKFORCE

LEADER'S NAME

_____

COLLECTION SLIP

Please make sure that you collect this slip when you bring your child each day. You will need it to collect your child at the end of the session. If your child is to be collected by someone else, please pass on this slip to that person.

   If you are unable to do this, or if your child is to go home on his/her own, please note this below, and return the slip to the registration desk immediately.

☐ Tick here if your child may go home alone.
☐ Tick here if someone else will collect your child.

Write that person's name next to the day concerned.

MONDAY _____
TUESDAY _____
WEDNESDAY _____
THURSDAY _____
FRIDAY _____

Please sign here if you have ticked either of the boxes above:

_____

Thank you for your cooperation.

Wastewatchers emergency phone number:

FRONT

If, when dropping off the child, the parent signs the reverse to say that their child may go home alone or with someone else, the registrars should give that slip to the child's Taskforce Leader during the session.

REVERSE

If a person wants to collect a child, but neither they nor the Taskforce Leader has the slip, they should be referred to the Holiday Club Leader, who will make sure that they are authorised to collect the child before allowing them to do so.

EVALUATION FORM

Use this evaluation form to review the session at **Wastewatchers.** Be open and honest about how you felt it went and include any suggestions you have for the next session. Adjust your material on the basis of your discoveries.

THE AIMS

Evaluate the aims for this session. Do you think the club as a whole, and your Taskforce Group in particular, achieved the aims for today? Why was this? Do you need to change anything for the next session?

CRAFT AND GAMES

Review these parts of the programme and consider how they fitted in with the rest of the day.
Craft:

Games:

ON THE TIP

How did the children react to the *On the tip* time?

Was there anything that was particularly successful?

Is there anything that needs rethinking?

THE CHILDREN

Which parts of the programme did the children react best to? Why do you think this was?

Think of each child. How did they respond to the teaching? Is there anything you need to do to help a specific child?

BIBLE TEACHING AND LITTLE GREEN PAGES/ECO SHEETS

How did the children respond to the Bible teaching and discussion you had around the story?

Did they enjoy it?

YOU

Identify any areas of the day that you were unhappy with. What problems did you see and what solutions can you offer to the rest of the team?

Do you have any general comments or suggestions for the next day?

Join us on our journey!

Many people tells us at Scripture Union about how they have used our holiday club material, what worked or what didn't, and how God blessed them in their club. We really welcome any feedback we receive and it excites us as we go on this journey together of sharing the good news of Jesus with children. If you could, we would love you to complete this form and send it to us. Alternatively, you could email us your responses to holidayclub@scriptureunion.org.uk

WASTEWATCHERS FEEDBACK FORM

Name

Address

Church name

Church address

Numbers of children at **Wastewatchers**

5 to 7s

8 to 11s

Other age groups (please specify)

In your opinion, what was the ratio of churched/non-churched children?

What comments do you have about how your club went?

What comments do you have about the **Wastewatchers** material?

What plans for following up **Wastewatchers** do you have? How will you keep in contact with the children and their families?

What two training needs do you think you have in your team

Is there any way Scripture Union could help you in your children's work?

☐ We would like to keep in touch with you by placing your name on our mailing list. If you would prefer not to be added, please tick the box.
SU does not sell or lease its mailing list.

What a load of rubbish!
The *Wastewatchers* Song

Words and Music by Trevor Ranger

Follow me

Alex Taylor and Helen Gale

In John 8 verse 12 Jesus said: 'I am the light for the world.' Fol-low me fol-low me and you won't be walk-ing in the dark, You will have the light, the light that gives life. Fol-low me fol-low me, and you will have the light, fol-low me fol-low me and you will have the light, fol-low me fol-low me, and you will have the light. You will have the light, the light that gives life.

PART 6

Wastewatchers Day by Day

PLANNING YOUR SESSION

When you come to plan each day, make sure you have read the descriptions of the programme in Part 1. Select the activities according to the children you are likely to have at the club. Use the evaluation form on page 50 at the end of each session to identify areas that might not be working well and to get ideas on how to change those areas.

You do not need to include all the activities listed here in your programme.

Making your choice

There are many factors which will influence your choice of activities:

- The children involved. The children should be the most important consideration when choosing the daily activities. Children respond differently to the same activity. Taskforce Leaders in particular should bear this in mind when planning their Taskforce time.
- The length of the club. Simply, if you have a long club, then you will be able to do more! The timings given are merely guidelines, different children will take different lengths of time to complete the same activity. Be flexible in your timings, judge whether it would be more valuable to complete an activity, even though it

may be overrunning, rather than cut it short and go on to the next activity. Have something in your programme you can drop if things overrun.

- The leaders available. Not every club will be able to find leaders with the necessary skills to fulfil every requirement. If you can't find anyone with a Basic Food Hygiene Certificate, you will have to limit the refreshments you can provide. If you don't have musicians, then you'll have to rely on backing tracks or miss out the singing. If you don't have anyone dramatic, you might have to miss out the drama.

To help Taskforce Leaders prepare for the Taskforce time, the questions for each day can be found in the **Wastewatchers** website.

Helpful symbols

Throughout the book, you will see these two symbols:

ALL TOGETHER
This logo indicates that all the children are together to do these activities.

TASKFORCE GROUPS
This logo indicates that these activities are to be done in Taskforce Groups.

Sunday service I

ALL-AGE SERVICE OUTLINE

Introduction
Show some photos of a church member as a baby, as a toddler, as a 5-year-old, as a teenager etc on an OHP or through a projector. How have they changed? What is different about them? This transformation has taken a long time! Not all transformations take so long, as will be discovered later in the service.

Song
Sing a couple of songs to celebrate how God is faithful throughout the years – such as 'Faithful one' or 'God's promises' (*Light for Everyone CD*, Scripture Union 2004).

Prayer
Invite everyone to call out things that have happened this week that they are thankful for. Write these down. Has anyone experienced change this week, such as a birth, or a death, job change, end of school year, house move? Thank God for what he has done and pray for those facing change.

Introducing Wastewatchers
The rest of the church needs to know what **Wastewatchers** is all about. However, if in this service you have lots of the children who are coming to the club, be careful just how much you share, because you do not want to spoil it for them. Teach everyone the **Wastewatchers** song and even try to sing it as a round.

You will want to explain something about the environmental aspect of the club and the Taskforce community project you have planned either during the club or at a later date. You could show part of the *A Rocha* video (on the **Wastewatchers** DVD), an inspirational example of how a rubbish tip was transformed into a country park. Alternatively, introduce this towards the end of the service after the Bible discovery.

Commission the leaders
If appropriate, interview one of the team leaders, to find out what they are looking forward to and what preparations they have been making.

Invite all the leaders who are taking part in the club to stand up. If possible pray for each of them by name (making sure that no one gets missed out or misnamed!). Ask for God to give each of them:
- his love for the children and for the rest of the team.

- his strength and energy for the demands of the club.
- his joy in serving him and seeing lives transformed

Read 2 Timothy 1:7: 'God's Spirit doesn't make cowards out of us. The Spirit gives us power, love and self-control.'

Invite all the children who are coming to the club to stand up. Ask God to give both team and children:
- protection so that no one is hurt or in danger.
- happiness in having fun during one of the best weeks of the year.
- listening ears to hear God's voice through the stories, the conversations and the whole **Wastewatchers** experience.

Prayer for the club
Ask the overall leader of the club to identify five specific prayer needs, which may be an expansion of the above points. Display these so that everyone can see them, or print them on a prayer card for people to take home to help them pray throughout the club.

Ask everyone to stand in small groups, although, if your church furniture allows for it, people may prefer to sit. In small groups, invite everyone to pray for these prayer points. Encourage the children to participate. This need not take long but provides everyone with an opportunity to contribute their prayer for the club. Try to ensure that team members are to be found in different groups.

Songs

Sing two or three of the songs you plan to sing during **Wastewatchers**.

Bible discovery

Either give a lump of clay or play dough to everyone or to people in groups or just have one large lump at the front. Explain that at the beginning of time there was nothing. But God changed all that, which the children will discover this week.

Read Genesis 2:4–11.
First ask everyone to turn the lump of clay into a person shape (verse 7 – God transformed soil or clay into a human being). Comment on what good attempts have been made. What can a human being do? (People should comment on good and bad things that we are capable of doing.)

Ask them to crush up their lump and then form a pear shape (verse 9 – God made fruit trees among other kinds of trees). The pear shape is a bit more demanding than an apple or orange. Again, admire people's efforts. What can you do with a pear or pear tree?

Ask them to change their pear shape into a rock shape. What can you do with a rock? (It may contain gold or precious stones (verse 12) but rocks can also destroy.)

God made a beautiful world for us to enjoy and to be part of. But all these things can become spoiled or misused. People can do wrong things and can use created things in a destructive way. God gave people the choice of whether or not to obey him. He told them not to eat from the fruit of the tree in the middle of the garden. The fruit of this tree would give them the ability to know the difference between right and wrong. They chose to disobey God.

That spoiled their beautiful relationship with God and the beauty of the world they lived in. From then on, people have needed to be changed again. That is a transformation that only God can make possible through what Jesus did on the cross. It's that transformation in us that can make the difference to the world we live in – that is what **Wastewatchers** is all about!

We are all looking forward to the time when God's work of changing those who love him, and changing the world, will be completed. Meanwhile, listen to what Paul wrote 2,000 years ago – read from Romans 8:18–22,38,39 in a child-friendly version. Wow!

This happened to me…

Briefly interview a team member about how their life has been transformed by what Jesus did on the cross for them. They could talk about what they are looking forward to when God's work is complete, either when they get to heaven or when Jesus returns. Make sure that they speak in jargon-free ways that make sense to people of all ages and backgrounds.

Community project

God also wants us to make a difference to his world by doing things to help the environment. As we are transformed, so God wants us to transform the world around us. Fill in the details of what you plan to do this week in the community project.

Song

Conclude with a song that recognises God's power or his love for us. For example:
'Over all the earth', 'God's love is deeper than the deepest ocean'.

Thank people for coming to the service and encourage everyone to pray for the club.

From nothing to something

AIMS FOR TODAY

To help all children feel settled, whether they have been to a holiday club before or not.

God's Word

- To discover what a beautiful world God made.
- To hint that all is not perfect in God's world. Human beings have been responsible for that. We have not always wanted to live as God wishes.

Word for us

- To wonder at God's beautiful world.
- To realise we have a responsibility to care for God's world and explore practical things we can do.
- To recognise that we have contributed to the lack of care in God's world.

Bible story

God creates the world and gives people the job of caring for it (Genesis 1).

Key word from John 1

'In the beginning was the one who is called the Word. The Word was with God and was truly God. From the very beginning the Word was with God. And with this Word, God created all things. Nothing was made without the Word. Everything that was created received its life from him…' (John 1:1–4a).

Today's session focuses on the fact that God created a good and beautiful world, something that all children can identify with. As the rubbish tip grows through the session, human disobedience will be hinted at. To introduce the two big themes of creation and fall in one session is very demanding for children who know little about the good news of the gospel, so concentrate on the wonder of God's creation. The effect of sin, the fall and God's forgiveness in Christ will be part of Day 3 and Day 4. Throughout Wastewatchers, our role in caring for God's world and living with the effects of sin will become clear.

The world of a child

All children are aware of ecological and environmental issues. It is part of the curriculum at school. All children have an innate capacity to wonder. They may appreciate the vastness and beauty of God's creation without actually knowing him as the creator. So those from a non-church background will feel very comfortable with the subject matter of today's session. Expect them to contribute on a level playing field with children who are already part of the church community.

There is no need to engage with issues of how the world came into being. Christians disagree about that and a holiday club aimed at reaching children with the good news of Jesus is not the context in which to discuss these issues. The question as to why there are so many things going wrong in the world is one that many children may not have consciously asked. It is important to explore what sin is and its effects. However, try to hold back from majoring on this unless it is obvious that a child wishes to talk about it.

GETTING READY

Rubbish tip

The tip is in the early stages of development. It will grow as the session progresses. If you are using the drama, you will simply want to have artificial green grass for the perfect lawn, a little rubbish, such as a mound of transportable garden rubbish, and a wheelie bin to the side. Hidden away will be other rubbish, such as an old bicycle, car tyre, old furniture, old carpet – anything that is big, non-toxic and safe!

If you are not doing the drama, devise a way of introducing the children to the tip and add extra bits as a sign of how we have misused God's world as a result of sin. During the programme you can discuss how the tip has changed at the start of each session. You could create a large background picture of a garden that is covered in graffiti as the day's session progresses.

Physical preparation

Talk through the session's programme, and make sure that everyone is aware of their responsibilities. Encourage the team to be as welcoming and interactive with the children as possible. Ask Taskforce Leaders to make sure that they speak some encouraging words to every child in their group. Ensure that all the resources are ready for the various activities.

Equipment checklist – Day 1
Security: registration forms, badges, pens, team lists

- **Binmen/women:** running order, notes, resources for **Wastewatchers** challenge and WWW, **Wastewatchers** DVD, plants for light experiment
- **Storyteller:** resources
- **Taskforce Groups:** resources for CLEARING THE GROUND, pens, Bibles, *Little Green Pages*, Eco Sheets, Bible discovery resources, Bible discovery notes
- **Creative prayer:** resources
- **Music:** music for your chosen songs, including the **Wastewatchers** song, *Learn and Remember verse* song, other background music
- **Drama:** props
- **Technology:** check PA, OHP/data projector and DVD player are all working and in focus
- **Games and craft:** all the resources for your chosen activities
- **Refreshments:** drinks and biscuits, or other snacks
- **Rubbish tip:** the start of the rubbish tip, including large, safe rubbish like an old bicycle or large tyres

Spiritual preparation

This first preparatory session should be mainly in small groups (directed by an overall leader) to encourage everyone to join in, discuss and pray together. If team members are already divided in age-group teams, stay in these groups in this session. Ask everyone to talk about what in creation they find most thrilling. Why did they choose that particular thing? Read Genesis 1:20–25 using *Little Green Pages*, and ask everyone to imagine what was happening. Talk together about what pictures they have in their mind – it is likely that everyone has different ideas! Read verse 25 out loud again. God was pleased with what he had created, very pleased.

Read Genesis 1:26–31. How would you put the task that God had given to men and women in words that children understand?

Spend some time praying in your

groups, thanking God for the beautiful world he has made. Then pray for one another.

Finally, read out John 1:1–3. Jesus, the Word, was in the beginning, involved in creation. Challenge the team to learn the whole of John 1:1–14 during the course of the club, using the same version, (ideally the CEV, which is in *Little Green Pages*).

CLEARING THE GROUND
(10 minutes)

Play some lively music and display the **Wastewatchers** logo to welcome the children as they arrive and are registered. The children are given their badge for the day and are taken to their Taskforce Groups to be introduced to their leaders.

Taskforce Groups

What you need

- Cress seeds, a shallow saucer and damp cotton wool – just one for the group
- Multi-coloured tissue paper or thin paper, strips of green paper, felt or wire for a flower stalk, large sheet of background paper, sticky tape, scissors, pencil or
- Finger paint, paper and pens

Everyone in the Taskforce Group begins to get to know each other by doing one of these activities.

Plant some seed

Sprinkle cress seeds on the dampened cotton wool and put in a safe place where it can be seen. Make sure it is dampened every day and see how it grows during the week. An ongoing example of transformation for each group! Note: you may want to adapt this suggestion if you are doing the Light experiment.

Flowers

Ask each child to choose their favourite colour of paper and create a flower using tissue paper and green stalk material. Gather a square of

tissue paper in the middle and secure with sticky tape. Stick a stalk to the taped section to create a flower. This could be a flower that already exists or they can invent one!

Insects

Invite children to create an insect (real or imaginary) by using fingerprints to make the body and head, and then adding legs, arms and feelers with a pen.

Stick these flowers and/or insects on background paper that can decorate your Taskforce Ground. (Give time for the children to go and wash their hands after finger painting.)

ON THE TIP
(35 minutes)

Play music as the children join the larger group. The Binmen/women welcome them to **Wastewatchers**. As it is the first day, explain how the morning programme works and any other things the children need to know. This will include telling them about what happens in the event of a fire, where the toilets are and any other 'rules' you may have, such as wearing your badge all the time or not leaving the building. Keep these 'rules' to a minimum. Introduce the bottle bank and say that this is where children can put any pictures, jokes or questions during the week. Say that you will show or read out some contributions each day.

Warm up

What you need

- Energetic music and a plan of movements for the children to follow

What you do

Lead a workout to music with a strong beat. The children will have fun and use up some energy. The lyrics of the song could have a connection to God's creation. As they sit down, draw attention to the tip.

Wastewatchers challenge

Everyone is involved in this challenge.

What you need

- A picture made up of lots of images of created things (you could use web items or items cut out of magazines and newspapers and stuck on a large sheet)
- Paper and pen for each Taskforce Group

What you do

Make sure children are sitting in their Taskforce Groups. Show the picture for 15 seconds and tell the children that, as soon as 15 seconds is up, they have one minute to write down all the created things that appeared on the screen. Check the answers and give the groups with the highest score a picture of something in creation to be put as decoration in their Taskforce Ground.

Songs

Introduce the first part of the **Wastewatchers** song. Sing other non-confessional songs, suitable to use with children who know little about Jesus.

Tell the story

Show Episode 1 from the DVD, in which God made a beautiful world but things began to go wrong.

Alternatively, tell the story in the following way or ask the children to make appropriate sound effects as you tell the story. You can do as much or as little as you want to in the retelling but you will need to practise!

What you need

- Gloomy music, sea music on CD plus sounds of movement, xylophone, wind in trees, animal sounds etc
- A giant sun and moon to hang down from the ceiling
- A pile of soil in a bucket
- A small flower or piece of grass for each child (consider which flowers would be appropriate to pick)
- Tree branches
- Pictures or models of fish, birds and animals – all as big as possible

What you do

Make the room as dark as possible without alarming any nervous children. Then start to tell the story:

Imagine you are surrounded by nothing, no one is anywhere near you. *(If you are in a large room with space, let the children find a space for themselves.)* Close your eyes and try to imagine what that would be like. And it is gloomy and dark. *(Play gloomy music.)* But in the middle of all this is God. He just is!

And as God moved around, he began to create. Out of nothing he began to separate things out. He made light different from dark. *(Ask everyone to open their eyes. Raise the lighting slightly and keep on doing this until God has made humans.)*

He made the sky different from the earth. *(Shine a moving spotlight over the ceiling.)*

He made the dry land different from the sea. Just listen to this. *(Play sea music or sound effects.)* Waves that crashed over the rocks, sea that swooshed up the coast, little waves that lapped on the beach.

And the dry land was like the soil in this bucket. *(Tip the soil onto the ground where all can see it.)* And God looked at what he had made and he was very pleased with everything. 'This is very good,' he said.

He made the sun and the moon and the stars. The sun was bright and glowing with blurred edges and it slowly moved across the sky. The moon was pale and silvery and it changed its shape as night followed night. It shone in the darkness. The stars were far away and mysterious, like tiny silver dots on a huge screen. *(Play a xylophone. Shine the spotlight on the sun and moon that are hanging from the ceiling.)* And God looked at what he had made and he was very pleased with everything. 'This is very good,' he said.

He created plants and flowers and trees to grow, all different. He created red, yellow, pink, blue, orange flowers: some had lots of petals, some had long stems, some had thorny stems; he created tall trees and short ones: some had rough, brown trunks, some had smooth, silvery trunks, some produced nuts, some produced soft fruit; he created bushes and grasses and reeds; he created vegetables that grew under the ground and vegetables that grew above the ground; he created wheat and maize and barley corn. *(Play wind sound effects. Give some grass or a flower to each child.)* Just look at the plant/grass, feel it, smell it, what do you notice about it? And God looked at what he had made and he was very pleased with everything. 'This is very good,' he said.

God created birds and fish and animals, all sorts, all different, some big, some small, some fast, some slow, some furry, some slimy, some bright-coloured, some dull-coloured, some fierce, some friendly. *(Play animal sound effects. Show the pictures or models of the animals.)* And God looked at what he had made and he was very pleased with everything. 'This is very good,' he said.

Finally, God created human beings. They were different from the animals because they were able to be friends with God. They could do all sorts of things with their bodies. They could clap, sniff, shout, whistle, make a tight fist shape, curl up into a small ball, thump their chest (carefully!) Tarzan-style. *(The children should try out all of these things. Ask them if they have any suggestions of their own.)* And God gave them a special job to do. He asked them to give names to all the animals. He also told them that they had to look after everything in the world. They had to make sure that fruit and vegetables grew properly, that trees grew properly, that the animals, birds and fish were well cared for. This was a big job but God knew that human beings could do this properly.

And God looked at what he had made and he was very pleased with everything. 'This is very good,' he said.

But things did not quite work out like that. Things have gone wrong in our world. (*Ask for ideas of pollution, famine, destruction of the rainforest and climate change – the children should have plenty to say.*)

Right at the beginning, the man and woman God had made decided that they did not always want to do what God wanted in the beautiful world he had given them to live in. They chose to disobey him. And, from then on, things went wrong. They began to fall out with each other and argue. They found it such hard work to look after the land and the animals, and they began to feel pain. God was still with them and they still looked after God's world but they didn't feel close to God. Not any more.

The world that God had made was still very good, but the bad things people did had messed it all up.

God did something about all that. We'll find out more during **Wastewatchers**.

Put the plant in the box and leave the other two plants on view.

Find the WasteWatcherWord (WWW)

Day 1 From nothing to something

What you need
- The WWW written in large letters on a long strip of paper, rolled up and put inside a large deflated balloon

What you do
Show the children the balloon. Then ask another leader to blow it up. As they do so, comment on how something which looks like nothing is getting bigger and bigger. Tie the balloon up and then 'notice' that there is something inside it. Ask any children who don't like loud noises to

cover up their ears, then burst the balloon. Show the strip of paper to them and comment on what is written on it.

Explain that this is today's WWW. There will be one each day. The WWW reminds us that each day something is being transformed into something else. **Wastewatchers** is all about change!

Introduce the **Wastewatchers** Environmental Project if you are going to do this (see page 18). Explain the details. In this project, we are changing the world around us and making it better. We are doing the task that God asked the first man and woman to do, looking after God's world.

Prayer for the world
Explain that Christians believe that God hears us when we talk to him. He loves to hear us saying thank you to him and loves to change things when we ask him, just like a good mum or dad loves to do. That's what prayer is. Each day we are going to pray for our world. If there is anything a child would like you to pray for, write it on a piece of paper and bring it to the Binmen/women. (This is a bit more serious than the jokes and pictures which will get put into the bottle bank so needs to be brought to the leaders!) Choose whatever you wish to pray for but at the start of the week it would be appropriate to thank God for parents and grandparents and pray for them at home or work while the children are at **Wastewatchers**. (If small children are showing evidence of homesickness, you may wish to amend this suggestion.)

Ask the children to close their eyes and picture their parents, grandparents and/or carers. Thank God for them and ask him to be close to them during **Wastewatchers**.

If you are going to conclude with 'Amen', explain that this means 'I agree'.

TASKFORCE
50 minutes

Refreshments
5 minutes
Serve refreshments to the children in small groups.

Bible discovery
15 minutes

With older children
If you are using *Little Green Pages* turn to page 6, or have enough copies of Genesis 1 for each child. Ask a confident reader to read Genesis 1:20–26. Ask each child to say which they like best from the general categories in the list: sea monsters, sea creatures, birds, tame animals, wild animals or reptiles. Why have they made their choice? Then read verse 25 altogether.

Pray together. Ask each child in turn to say the following words, filling in the name of their favourite animal/bird etc:

'Thank you God that you made
_____'

After each child has spoken, everyone says together:

'God saw that everything was very good.'

Do the puzzles on pages 10–12 in *Little Green Pages*. You will need to read Genesis 1:27–31. If you have time and you have some able readers in the group, read Genesis 3:1–23.

With younger children
Read out loud Genesis 1:20–27, asking the children to listen out for their favourite type of animal, maybe a wild one, or a bird or a fish. Do the Eco Sheet together (see page 65).

With all ages groups
Adapt these questions and discussion starters for use with your group:
- Talk about the wonder of the world God has made. Let the children share their enthusiasms.

- What things have gone wrong in the world? Share with them that God never intended that things should go wrong.
- What reasons were given in the story about why things went wrong? (You may need to remind the children if you have not read Genesis 3.)
- What did God want people to do in the world?
- Talk about what you are going to do in your community to make a difference.

Games

15 minutes

The theme of all these games is creation. Use one or more in your games session.

Physical strength circus

This is an opportunity to show what fantastic things we can do with our bodies, the bodies that God created. Be sensitive to any child with a physical disability.

What you need

- A means of scoring and a watch/clock with a second hand per group
- One or a combination of these things: skipping ropes (enough for each person in one group), hula hoops (enough for each person in one group), bench (for jumping on and off), gym floor mat (for somersaults or handstands), netball hoop and ball, football and goal

What you do

Split the children into groups with one leader. Mixed ability groups will be fairer if the groups compete against each other but this will not help age-based Taskforce Groups get to know each other. Alternatively, children can 'compete' within their Taskforce Group.

Devise a variety of timed activities (about four minutes each) that test physical strength and cater for a variety of skills for both genders. You will need to work out how to award a score for each activity. Each group tries each activity in the circus in turn. Each child's score or the whole group's score is recorded.

This has to be well organised and fast-moving. Impress upon the leaders their need to concentrate on keeping their group moving.

What animal am I?

This demonstrates the variety of the animals and birds God has made. Devise other animal games such as putting the tail on the donkey or a beetle drive (with a variety of animals or insects split into six parts, one part for each dice number).

What you need

- Set of cards with the name of an animal on each card, either written or as a picture depending upon the age of the children – there should be at least two cards for each animal: eg owl, cuckoo, duck, cockerel, crow, kangaroo, elephant, cow, sheep, horse, dog, cat, mouse, gorilla. A good reference book is *Sharing Nature with Children* Vol 1 Joseph Cornell (Sharing Nature Foundation).

What you do

Give a card to each child. They must not show the card to anyone else. Each child makes the noise or action of their animal and goes in search of other children sharing their animal.

Craft

15 minutes

Nature/conservation mobiles

What you need

- Two pieces of dowling/pieces of wood (the same size and able to connect together in a cross shape) for each child
- Plain card
- Templates of animals, fish, birds; shapes that depict environmental concerns connected with marine,

urban and woodland life
- Coloured string, wool or fishing wire
- Paint, glitter glue, felt-tips etc to decorate the template
- Hole punch

What you do

Using the template, the children choose and cut out the shapes/pictures in card. They can create their own shapes if they wish. The children should colour/decorate the shapes as they wish, then punch a hole in the top of each one.

Using string of varied length, tie the shapes to the crossed dowling, which could itself be covered with crêpe paper.

> In the trial, an urban group used pictures of a dolphin, an oil drum, a graffiti wall and broken glass

An alternative to this for older children is to create a bird, with a body cut out of stiff card, and the wings attached at 90° to the body with a hole punched in the body to allow it to be suspended with string. The body can be covered with feathers, or other material. Over a couple of days papier mâché could be put on the body to make it more substantial. Once this is dried it could be painted. Children will have to work out the dynamics of the wing span which makes it more of a challenge. The birds could be hung up for the rest of the holiday club.

Other suggestions

- Make something from nothing using clay, possibly clay people which children can hold in their hands just as God holds us in his hands.
- Stained glass biscuits – a boiled sweet in the centre surrounded by biscuit mix and baked.
- Make a big bird banner – using coloured paper draw around children's hands, cut out the shapes and stick onto a large bird shape to form feathers.

The trial planned for older children to make bird boxes over the course of the week. These were to be given to the local school and put up in the churchyard. Several helpers on the fringe of church gave time to make this possible.

BIG CLEAN UP
30 minutes

Bottle bank

Sing one or two songs as the children arrive and read out a few prepared jokes, encouraging children to put their own pictures or jokes in the bottle bank. Some children may have already put some things in the bottle bank!

Bird Life, the RSPB's junior magazine, is a good source of good and bad wildlife jokes!

Quiz

Keep this short to remind everyone of the story and explore some fantastic animal facts.

Score by giving each child who answers correctly an animal-shaped sweet or any other suitable prize such as an animal sticker. For example:
- What did God make first/second?
- What is today's WWW? (From nothing to something)

In addition, here is a Wildlife Wow Quiz (correct answers in bold):

Q There are seven vertebrae in your neck. How many are there in a giraffe's neck?

A **7**, 25, 82

Q You have 12 pairs of ribs. How many pairs does a big snake have?

A 12, About 120, **About 400** (The tiny blindsnake has nearly 600!)

Q Which bird migrates the furthest?

A Ostrich, Swallow, **Arctic tern** (Some travel 11,000 miles between their breeding grounds and their wintering area, and then 11,000 miles back again.)

Q What is the longest insect in the world?

A Goliath beetle, **Giant walking stick**, Ladybird (The record is a female stick insect that was 55.5 cm long)

Q What is the world's biggest fish?

A **Whale shark**, Angler fish, Goldfish (A whale shark can be over 15 metres long and weigh over 16 tonnes. Its mouth can measure 1.5 m wide, but it only eats plankton. The angler fish has a fin like a long fishing rod growing from its snout, which glows to lure prey towards the mouth of the fish and then, snap, they are eaten!)

Q What animal lives the longest?

A An elephant, A skunk , **A tortoise** (A Madagascar radiated tortoise lived at least 188 years.)

Q What bird can fly backwards?

A Kestrel, **Hummingbird**, Penguin (Hummingbirds can fly upside-down too. There are over 300 species of hummingbird.)

Q Which bird has the biggest wingspan?

A Andean Condor, Blue tit, **Wandering albatross** (3.5m)

Q What is the fastest animal on land?

A **Cheetah**, Garden snail, Kangaroo (It can reach speeds of up to 70 mph!)

Q What is the world's biggest living animal?

A African Elephant, **Blue Whale**, Badger (The heaviest blue whale weighed 171 tonnes and was over 27 metres long.)

Drama

This introduces the drama characters and sees the rubbish in the park reaching its worst!

This happened to me…

Invite a team member to be interviewed or to share what they have done to change the environment for the better. This not only gives an opportunity to talk about the **Wastewatchers** project but also for them to talk about how they know that this is God's beautiful world and he wants us to care for it, even though there are things wrong in the world. Ask them about their favourite bird, tree etc. At the end, ask them what they like best about today's story. Make sure that what they say is in simple, child-friendly language and uses the phrases about God's world and our responsibility that you have been using all this session. Read page 31 for more suggestions.

Learn and remember

Begin to teach the children John 8:12. Remind them that in the beginning there was darkness everywhere, but God made light. Jesus took part in creation and he said he himself was light. You will find out more about that later in the week. But for today, learn this section: "Jesus said, 'I am the light for the world!'" You could work out some simple hand actions for this. Alternativey, start to teach the *Learn and remember verse* song (see page 53).

Ask the children what it would be like always to live in night-time with no light. You may be surprised at their suggestions. This will impress on the children why light matters and help them make links with what Jesus came to do and be. If you are doing the light experiment you could refer to that at this point.

If you want a different memory verse each day, Psalm 24:1 is a good summary of today's theme, although note the centrality of the *Learn and remember verse* to the **Wastewatchers** teaching programme.

The light experiment

Remind the children that God created light right at the beginning. Introduce the three plants (all the same size) and explain that over the course of the club you are going to conduct a science experiment. One plant you are going to put in a dark box/cupboard where you will water it but otherwise it will get no light or attention. The second plant you are going to leave in the room where it will be watered and that is all. The third plant is going to have specialist treatment. It is going to be tricked into thinking that there are two daytimes every 24 hours because a timed light is going to be shone on it for two hours every night. You are going to see if the extra light gives extra life so that it grows more quickly.

Creative prayer idea

What you need

- The picture used for the **Wastewatchers** challenge

What you do

Show the images and ask the children to pick out just one of them that they would like to thank God for. Tell the children that you are going to talk with God. Explain that we do not have to put our hands together or close our eyes when we talk with him but we do have to be still so we can listen and

not distract other people. Explain too that if they agree with what you have said, they can say 'Amen' at the end. Ask the children to make their hands into the shape of the animal they have chosen – wing-shaped, fish-shaped or head-shaped for an animal (an elephant needs to have an arm used as a trunk!). Ask the children to say out loud the name of their chosen animal when you raise your arm.

'Father God, we thank you for all the wonderful things in your world: the trees, the flowers, the hills, the streams, the sea and all the animals, birds, insects and fish. We thank you especially for (*Raise your arm.*) _____.

We are sorry that your world has been spoilt, but help us to do our part to care for it. Thank you that we can be part of **Wastewatchers**. Amen.

TASKFORCE TOO
5 minutes

Spend the last five minutes of the club in Taskforce Groups, finishing off any craft or puzzles from *Little Green Pages*. Taskforce Leaders should take this opportunity to chat about the day's Bible story, asking the children what they found out, as well as asking the children what they thought.

Taskforce Leaders should also make sure they know how each child is getting home. As each child is leaving, they should say goodbye and remind them about the next session.

FINAL CLEAR-UP

After the children have left and the clear-up is over, gather the team together for a time of reflection, comment and prayer. You may wish to use the evaluation form on page 50.

> If you are going to run an environmental **Wastewatchers** project during the holiday club week, get it launched early in the week so that enthusiasm can gain momentum!

From nothing to something

In this maze, go past all the things that God has made. Begin at the beginning. Then label each section you pass with the number day it was created.

Fill in the missing words

God looked at what he had done.

All of it was _ _ _ _   _ _ _ _.
(Genesis 1:31)

My favourite!

My favourite animal/bird is _____.

It is _____ (colour)

It has _____ (number) legs.

It makes a _____ sound.

It lives _____.

I like it because _____ _____.

Draw your favourite animal or bird here.

Dear God, thank you for everything you have made, especially

DAY

2

From water into wine

AIMS FOR TODAY

To develop the relationships that began yesterday and to welcome any new children.

God's Word

- To discover that Jesus came into the world to help people when things seemed impossible – that's why he could come to the rescue at the wedding.
- To introduce Jesus as God himself, who is able to perform miracles.

Word for us

- To explore how Jesus is with us all the time and can help us when things seem impossible. This is a person whom children can come to love.

Bible story

Jesus changes water into wine (John 2:1–12).

Key word from John 1

'The Word became a human being and lived here with us. We saw his true glory, the glory of the only Son of the Father. From him all the kindness and all the truth of God have come down to us' (John 1:14).

The world of a child

This is a very ordinary situation. Most children know something about weddings, even though customs in the Middle East 2,000 years ago were a bit different. Here is Jesus, God in a human body, who is doing ordinary things. For some children this in itself runs counter to what they are led to believe about God. Other faiths certainly do not have scope for God to take on a human form.

Not only did Jesus help people in need and do something miraculous, he also saved the organisers from being shamed for running out of refreshments. Things going wrong (often in ways that seem unfair) and being embarrassed are common emotions for children. Let them imagine what it was like in this wedding.

This same Jesus is alive today, by his Spirit, and therefore it is possible for us to know him and allow him to make the impossible possible. Jesus' death and resurrection are the focus for Days 4 and 5, but today's story plants the seed thought that Jesus is still alive! Personal stories about how Jesus is with us now are an important means of helping children understand what this means.

GETTING READY

Rubbish tip

Much more rubbish has arrived since yesterday, including an old bath or container for water. In the drama, this will become a pond. This also ties in with the water theme of the day.

Physical preparation

Talk through the session's programme, and make sure that everyone is aware of their responsibilities. Encourage the team to be as welcoming and interactive with the children as possible. Ask Taskforce Leaders to make sure that they speak some encouraging words to every child in their group. Ensure that all the resources are ready for the various activities.

Equipment checklist – Day 2

- **Security:** registration forms, badges, pens, team lists
- **Binmen/women:** running order, notes, resources for **Wastewatchers** challenge and WWW, **Wastewatchers** DVD, plants from light experiment
- **Storyteller:** resources
- **Taskforce Groups:** resources for CLEARING THE GROUND, pens, Bibles, *Little Green Pages* or Eco Sheets, five large paper speech bubbles, Bible discovery notes
- **Creative prayer:** resources
- **Music:** music for your chosen songs, including the **Wastewatchers** song, *Learn and remember verse* song, other background music
- **Drama:** props

- **Technology:** check PA, OHP/data projector and DVD player are all working and in focus
- **Games and craft:** all the resources for your chosen activities
- **Refreshments:** drinks and biscuits, or other snacks
- **Rubbish tip:** more rubbish, including an old bath or large water container

Each team member could wear a buttonhole because they are going to a wedding. Each child could be given a small flower to put behind their badge because they too are going to a wedding.

Spiritual preparation

Ask everyone to share one thing that happened yesterday that they want to thank God for. Spend time praising God for who he is and what he did for you all during Day 1.

Read John 2:1–12. Just imagine how desperate the family must have felt. What words describe their feelings? Had this disaster happened because a mistake had been made or was it unavoidable? Ask people to comment on this. We don't know, but what is important is that Jesus was there and he made all the difference. He changed a situation from potential shame to honour!

Invite everyone to picture their group in their Taskforce Ground. Can they imagine Jesus there with them? Ask team members to pray quietly for each child by name, knowing that Jesus is there, even if they cannot remember everyone's face. Invite a couple of people to pray for you all in the light of the next session.

You will want to encourage people to learn the second part of John 1:1–14. Notice how verse 14 relates to today's story.

Some holiday clubs encourage the children to give to a charity that is featured throughout the week. If you

are going to do this, it needs to be introduced on Day 2. You could focus on an environmental charity. A Rocha has helped develop **Wastewatchers** with Scripture Union and would be one charity to consider. For details see pages 94-95 or visit www.arocha.org. Alternatively, you could feature a charity that works with street kids who literally live on a rubbish tip. Scripture Union in Peru does a great deal of work among such children.

CLEARING THE GROUND
10 minutes

Play some lively music and display the **Wastewatchers** logo to welcome the children as they arrive and are registered. The children are given their badge for the day and go to their Taskforce Groups. This is an opportunity for Taskforce Leaders to get to know the children better and find out what they enjoyed yesterday.

Taskforce Groups

What you need

- Felt-tip pens/crayons and a giant rubbish picture (page 54) or
- Various junk to create a model, sticky tape, scissors or
- Flower making materials (see Day 1) to make wedding buttonholes

Make any new children especially welcome and ask if any of your group can fill the newcomers in on what happened on Day 1. Any children who have brought jokes, pictures or questions should drop them in the bottle bank. Each group should spend time together on one or more of these activities:

Giant rubbish picture

On page 54, there is a rubbish picture for the groups to colour in. Enlarge to A3 or larger, to enable the whole group to work on the same picture. With this activity, it is not the colouring that is important (although

the children will, of course, want to have a good end product), but the conversations you have as you colour, and the sense of being a group as you work together.

> Some of the best conversations that have been had in children's work are when children's workers and children are just chilling out together, not doing anything very significant or meaningful. But a picture related to the theme of the club does raise issues that can be talked about. Colouring for the sake of it though is a lost opportunity. Encourage team members to pray for the children as they colour together, making the most of the time just to chat!

Junk modelling

During the drama, the characters work together to create beautiful and useful things from rubbish, and the Taskforce Groups can do the same! Decide together what you are going to create and then work together to produce it. Again, this is an important time for chatting to the children as you work.

Buttonholes

Follow the instructions in Day 1's CLEARING THE GROUND to produce buttonholes for the children to wear throughout the session. Be careful of sharp points.

ON THE TIP
35 minutes

The Binmen/women welcome the children to **Wastewatchers**, especially any new children. Remind the children that they can put any jokes, pictures or questions in the bottle bank.

Warm up

What you need

- Energetic music and a plan of movements for the children to follow

What you do

Lead a workout to music with a strong beat. The children will have fun and use up some energy. As they sit down, ask them what they notice about the tip.

Wastewatchers challenge

What you need

- Waterproofing for the floor and anything else that needs it
- An empty large clear plastic bottle and a beaker for every participating Taskforce Group (placed at different points around the room)
- A bucket of coloured water placed centrally

What you do

Each group sends one person to take part. Each person runs to scoop up a beaker of coloured water and pours it into the plastic bottle. At the end of the allocated time, the whistle blows and the winner is the person who has transferred the most liquid from the bucket to their bottle. Encourage groups to noisily support their representative.

This activity introduces the idea of transferring liquid, which leads onto the Bible story.

Songs

Introduce the verse of the **Wastewatchers** song. Also sing other non-confessional songs, suitable to use with children who know little about Jesus.

Tell the story

Show Episode 2 from the DVD, in which Jesus comes to the rescue at a wedding and turns water into wine.

Alternatively, tell the story in the following way:

One leader dresses up as Jesus' mother, Mary, wearing a carnation in a buttonhole or some other visually obvious or funny piece of wedding finery! She is in such a state because she has just come from the wedding in Cana (just 10 km from where they live). She tells the story.

During the story, emphasise what a great wedding it was, how well planned, that it had lasted several days already but sometimes the most unexpected things happen and they ran out of wine. It was so rude to stop serving people wine and so embarrassing for the groom and his family.

Mary mentioned the problem to Jesus, but she had no idea what exactly he would do. He ordered the servants to fill the six huge water jars that were used in a religious ceremony with water. They did what he said.

Then Jesus ordered them to put some of the liquid inside the jars into a glass and take it to the man in charge. Mary watched all this and wondered what on earth was going on. Did Jesus really know what he was doing?!

The man in charge licked his lips with sheer pleasure after one sip. This was the best wine ever, not the poorest of quality usually served at the end. The groom and his family were saved from embarrassment and were even complimented on the wine that they had saved till last!

Another alternative is to use this drama script:

Characters

Amos – a sleeping husband at a wedding
A wife – guest at a party
A waiter
The comedy comes in the switching of glasses. Amos is asleep in a chair. He has an empty glass in his hand and every so often snores or makes an unusual noise. His wife is sat on a chair beside him, staring into her empty glass, looking bored and occasionally staring around the room at other (*imaginary*) guests. She speaks with a northern English accent, as Galilee is in the north of the country.

Wife: Well Amos, I have to say, this wedding has been a disappointment. Look at the two of us, sat here, empty glasses for over half an hour and nothing to drink. Well, of course, how embarrassing. I mean, put on a party and run out of wine so soon. You wouldn't believe it really would you. (*Looks at Amos and shouts.*) Would you? Oh Amos, wake up will you. (*Shakes Amos. Amos stirs briefly and then settles back into sleep.*) That wedding we went to last week, well that was amazing. The wine flowed all night. It was a great party. But this… Talk about embarrassing. (*To Amos.*) You're an embarrassment as well you know. Oh yes, my husband, fast asleep at a wedding. Well, (*Pauses for a second.*) not that I blame you really. I'm a bit bored myself. I hope the wine comes out soon. (*Waiter enters with a jug of red liquid.*)
Waiter: Evening madam. More wine? (*Fills up the glass.*) And for the gentleman? (Fills up Amos' glass.) Enjoy the wine madam, you won't be disappointed. (*Waiter exits.*)
Wife: Oh, Amos! (*Elbows her husband.*) Amos, wake up! (*Takes a sip of wine.*) OOOOH, Amos, it's lovely! (*Drinks more.*) Oi! Wake up you lazy oaf, this party's looking up! (*Finishes her glass of wine and swaps glasses with Amos. She then starts to drink his wine.*) This really is amazing!
(*Waiter enters again with the jug.*)
Waiter: More wine, sir? He must have enjoyed it madam, he's finished it already! (*Waiter fills up Amos' glass and tops up the wife's glass too, then leaves the stage.*)
Wife: (*Finishing her glass of wine and swapping with Amos.*) Now I'm a bit puzzled. (*She starts to drink Amos' wine.*) Last week's wedding was

grand. But as the evening went on, the wine got more and more tasteless, didn't it, Amos? (Pokes him.) Not that we cared of course. (*She hiccups.*) But this wine, this is the best I've ever tasted. And it came out last of all!! Very strange.
(*Waiter enters and fills Amos' glass again.*)
Waiter: Finished again sir? You really do like this new wine!
Wife: Now young man, there is something I don't understand. We've been sat here for ages with empty glasses and long faces cos there was no wine. Then all of a sudden you come and give us the best wine I've ever tasted! How can that be?
Waiter: Well it's all down to Jesus. You know Jesus? The carpenter. Mary's son.
Wife: Mary? I know her.
Waiter: Well, Jesus filled up our big jars with water and said a prayer. Then instead of water coming out of the jars, out came this wonderful, beautiful, amazing red wine that you're drinking. I don't understand, but I know a miracle has happened. (*Waiter leaves the stage.*)
Wife: Amos, wake up! You need to hear this story. It's all about Jesus. You know the son of Mary. He changed water into wine.

© *Ruth Wills, Phil Brown*

Find the WasteWatcherWord (WWW)

From water into wine

What you need
- Pile of cardboard boxes
- Sheets of paper, marker pen
- Water pistol

What you do
Build a pile out of cardboard boxes and stick a sheet of paper with a dash for each letter in the WWW on each box. (You'll need 17 in total). Invite the children to call out one letter at a time. Every letter that is in the WWW is written on its dash. For every letter that is not, squirt water either at a volunteer leader or into the children themselves. How wet are they going to get?

Pray for the world

Continuing the water theme, find out about a part of the world where there is a water shortage or where a relief agency is building wells or other forms of irrigation. Or find out about the effects of a water shortage on wildlife in the UK. Tell the children about it. You may have been squirting water liberally just a few moments ago but now you want to explain the preciousness of water in places where there is a shortage. Ask the children to cup their hands to imagine that they are holding a few drops of precious water. Then briefly ask God to provide enough water and to help those conserving water supplies.

Alternatively, pray for people or situations the children have already mentioned or pray for the charity you are raising money for this week.

TASKFORCE
50 minutes

Refreshments
5 minutes

(You may want to delay serving refreshments until after *Little Green Pages*.)
Serve the children their refreshments in Taskforce Groups. Eating and drinking is a sociable thing especially as today's story is about a wedding. To continue the wedding theme, serve some fancy foods or nibbles, the sort you might get at a wedding. Serve a variety of drinks with different colours and use coloured straws. Thinking about wine, you could serve grape juice.

> If you have a group of older children, they could create their own exotic non-alcoholic cocktails, the sort that you might get at a wedding! Watch out for allergies!

Bible discovery
15 minutes

With older children
If you are using *Little Green Pages* turn to pages 20–21, or have enough copies of John 2:1–11 for each child who is going to read. Ask one child to read the part of Mary, one to be Jesus, one to be the man in charge of the feast and the most confident to be the narrator. Write in a speech bubble each of the speeches made by Mary, Jesus and the man in charge of the feast. (Only include the last few words of the man in charge in verse 10.) Give these bubbles out – a child holds up their bubble when the relevant part of the story is read.
Explore the story using the questions below, adapting them to yourself and your group. Then do the puzzles on pages 22–23.

With younger children
Read out loud from the Bible this story from John 2:1–11 before you have refreshments. Give out empty cups. Only fill them after you have explored the story and helped them to understand what an amazing thing Jesus had done! Complete the Eco Sheet after that.

With all children
Adapt these questions and discussion starters for use with your group:
- Talk about the sort of things that go wrong at a wedding. (Give examples you know.) Refer to the empty cups, if you are using them, and how disappointed you would be if there were no drinks today! You could also explore what makes the children embarrassed.
- How would you have felt if you were the bridegroom at this wedding?

- How would you have felt if you were the bridegroom when you realised what Jesus had done?
- What do you think Jesus' disciples and Mary were thinking about Jesus as they walked home at the end of the wedding?
- Give personal experience of how Jesus helped you when you had a problem.
- Think of things that the children have found difficult recently. Then ask God to help them with this difficulty. They could write it down, or draw it and hold the piece of paper as you pray for them.

Games
15 minutes

If it is possible, go outside to play these water games! These games reinforce the details of the story. You will need to check that parents are happy for their children to get wet!

Six pots relay

What you need
- Six beakers /pots for every team filled with water and a bucket per team
- 6 posts or markers

What you do
Divide the children into teams of seven and devise a circular route like a rounders pitch with six posts, positioning one child per team at each post. You will need two children to remain at Post A, the start.
The first child in each team begins at Post A carrying a beaker of water, which they pass onto the second child at Post B who runs to the third at Post C etc. The child at Post F empties their beaker into the bucket back at the start, Post A. The remaining child at Post A picks up the second beaker and runs to the first child who is now at post B etc.
The game finishes when all six beakers have been carried around the course and emptied into the bucket.

In a small space the children can do this one team at a time to see who completes it the quickest. In an open space, the teams can race each other. You could do this more than once! Remind the children that there were six pots at the wedding Jesus went to, which were huge and had to be filled up.

Alternative relays

1 Split the children into teams with half of every team at one end of the room/play area and half at the other and try one of these games:
- A child pats a balloon filled with water along the ground.
- A plastic bottle filled with water is rolled along.

2 Spread each team in a line the length of the area then try some of these games:
- Pass a plastic cup of water from one end to the other and back.
- Pass a plastic cup over the head of one child and between the legs of the next.

You could partially fill a balloon with water, one for every team, to make a 'water bomb' and use that for all the games!

> The wedding theme is a minor part of this story but with younger children and with just a small group, you might invite them to play at dressing up for a wedding! Remind them that Jesus came to help people when things went wrong at a wedding.

Craft
15 minutes

As you make these crafts, talk about the story and how Jesus did the impossible.

Wine jars

What you need
- Air-dry clay
- Modelling tools (proper clay tools or

improvised ones, such as plastic knives, cocktail sticks or spoons)
- Decorative materials, such as sequins, stickers or paint

What you do
Make cylindrical pots by rolling out and cutting a circular clay base. Roll out and cut a rectangular piece of clay. Place this upright on the base and curve around the edge to create the side of the pot. Alternatively, build up the side by winding long sausages of clay around the edge of the base. If you are able, allow these to dry before the children decorate them – you could do this craft over two days if you don't have the time in one session.

Party invitations

What you need
- A5 sheets of thin card
- Art materials

What you do
Give the children the card and whatever art materials you are using and ask them to create a wedding invitation to the wedding at Cana. This is a good way to talk about the story and explore what the children made of it. Let them use their imaginations to create their invitation. You might find out a lot about their impressions of the Bible passage from the invitations themselves!

Other craft ideas
- Design and make a wedding hat with a competition at the end for the best! (Don't do this craft if you intend to make hats on Day 5.)

 **BIG CLEAN UP**
30 minutes

Bottle bank

Sing one or two songs as the children arrive and read out any suitable jokes, display pictures and answer any questions that have been posted in the bottle bank.

Quiz

Have a quick multiple choice quiz to remind children of the details of the story. If you have people skilled in PowerPoint in your team, you could present the possible answers as they do in some quiz shows! Score by giving each child who answers correctly a piece of fruit or a flower to go behind their badge.

Possible questions

Q Where was the wedding that Jesus went to?

A Connor, **Cana**, Cayman, Cardiff

Q Who told Jesus they had run out of wine?

A **His mother**, his sister, his friend, his auntie

Q How much water did the six water jars hold in total?

A 100 litres, 300 litres, **600 litres**, 10,000 litres

Q How did the man in charge of the feast test new wine?

A Smelt it, dipped his finger in it, **sipped it**, spat it out

Q How did the man in charge of the feast describe the wine?

A Poor, watery, OK, **the best**

Q What was today's WWW?

A From darkness into light, **from water into wine**, from strength into   sweetness, from white into red

Drama

The park keeper is depressed because there is so much mess. But the young people offer to help him clear it up. There is so much that they decide to recycle it instead. They create a pond from an old bath. Instead of a pond, if you have limited space, you could make a bird bath.

This happened to me…

Invite a team member to be interviewed or to share their story of how Jesus came to help them when they were in a difficult situation.

Begin the interview by asking about their favourite drink, what they wore at the last wedding they went to etc to demonstrate to the children how normal they are! Then ask them what they like best about today's story. Make sure that what they say about Jesus is simple and in child-friendly language. Read pages 30–31 for more suggestions.

Learn and remember

If you are using just one memory verse, teach the children the second part of John 8:12: 'Jesus said, "I am the light for the world!. Follow me…"'

Continue learning the *Learn and remember verse* song!

If you are having a different verse each day, John 2:25 would fit with today's story: 'No one had to tell Jesus what people were like. He already knew.'

Light experiment

Show the children the two plants (but not the darkened one) and discuss if there is any difference yet. Remind them that you are testing to see if light gives life!

Creative prayer idea

The children take up a different position with each of the three stages of this prayer.

They sit cross-legged with closed eyes and think about something that has gone wrong for them recently. You could make a couple of suggestions. (They should have thought about this already in Taskforce Groups.)

They kneel on the floor, eyes closed, hands folded and ask God the Father to change that situation.

They stand up and stretch their arms as high as they can and shout out saying these two phrases after the leader, 'Thank you God! You have heard our prayer!'

TASKFORCE TOO
5 minutes

Spend the last five minutes of the club in Taskforce Groups, finishing off any craft or puzzles from *Little Green Pages*. Taskforce Leaders should take this opportunity to chat about the day's Bible story, asking the children what they found out, as well as asking them what they thought.

Taskforce Leaders should also make sure they know how each child is getting home. As each child is leaving, they should say goodbye and remind them about the next session.

FINAL CLEAR UP

After the children have left and the clear-up is over, gather the team together for a time of reflection, comment and prayer. You may wish to use the evaluation form on page 50.

For suggestions for suitable family and community activities see page 35. A 'wedding' banquet would be a great way to follow up today's theme!

From water into wine

The man in charge of the wedding called the bridegroom over and said, 'You have kept the best wine until last!' This was Jesus' first miracle. John 2:10,11

Can you spot eight differences between these two pictures of the wedding?

Jesus came to help the people at the wedding when they had a problem. Write or draw something in these jars that you find difficult.

Now ask Jesus to help you.

If you can only think of one thing to write or draw, colour the other jar in!

From darkness to light

DAY 3

AIMS FOR TODAY

To look for opportunities to talk with children about what they are discovering about Jesus. The children will be familiar with how the club is organised while relationships and trust between children and leaders will have increased.

God's Word

• To hear how the blind man was able to see and put his trust in Jesus, the one who is light for the world.
• To realise that the Pharisees, who had so much going for them, were actually the blind ones, living in darkness. They refused to accept the light for the world.

Word for us

• To explore how we are all like the Pharisees, in darkness, but Jesus can shine light and hope which gives us life.
• To explain a bit more about how things went wrong when the first man and woman disobeyed God.

Bible story

Jesus gives sight to the blind man and helps him trust in Jesus (John 9:1–41).

Key word from John 1
'The light keeps shining in the dark, and darkness has never put it out … The true light that shines on everyone was coming into the world' (John 1:5,9).

The emphasis of this session is on darkness to light, rather than on blindness and sight, although that inevitably is part of the story.

The world of a child

Many children are afraid of the dark, either because of the unknown or the imagined. They feel vulnerable, or something scary may have actually happened to them in the dark. This makes the idea of Jesus bringing light into darkness all the more powerful. The fact that he enabled a blind man to see is a great example of his love for individuals, meeting them where they most needed him. For many children, this will be sufficiently new and challenging.

Non-churched children will be less familiar with the idea that, metaphorically, we are all 'dark inside'. Basically we do not want to accept the light of Jesus that shows up our natural inclination to disobey God – sin. Be very careful how you use language during today's session. Avoid the word 'black' or 'naughty', for black to mean bad is inappropriate in our multiracial society and sin is far more than doing naughty things. It is all about being out of relationship with God. Since he is the source of all light, anything that is not part of him is therefore dark.

Again, the power of Jesus to bring about change is clear throughout the session. You will be preparing children to understand something of the meaning of Jesus' death on the cross.

On the first day there was some discussion about how things have gone wrong in the world and people disobeyed God. Children may remember this and it is a way of exploring the effects of sin.

GETTING READY

Rubbish tip

The tip is getting smaller (although rubbish is still around) and the pond or birdbath should be complete. This time a park bench is going to be introduced.

Physical preparation

Talk through the session's programme, and make sure that everyone is aware of their responsibilities. Encourage the team to be as welcoming and interactive with the children as possible. Ask Taskforce Leaders to make sure that they speak some encouraging words to every child in their group. Ensure that all the resources are ready for the various activities.

Equipment checklist – Day 3
Security: registration forms, badges, pens, team lists
Binmen/women: running order, notes, ten short recorded sounds of night noises for **Wastewatchers** challenge, resources for WWW, **Wastewatchers** DVD, plants from light experiment
Storyteller: resources
Taskforce Groups: resources for CLEARING THE GROUND, pens, Bibles, *Little Green Pages* or Eco sheets, Bible discovery notes
Creative prayer: resources
Music: music for your chosen songs, including the **Wastewatchers** song, *Learn and remember verse* song, other background music
Drama: props

Technology: check PA, OHP/data projector and DVD player are all working and in focus
Games and craft: all the resources for your chosen activities
Refreshments: drinks and biscuits, or other snacks
Rubbish tip: more rubbish, including two old chairs and two planks to make a bench, paint

Spiritual preparation

Light a candle at the start of your time together to remind you that today's theme is Jesus, the light for the world. Split the group into two giving each a large piece of paper and a felt-tip pen. Read out John 9:1–41, asking each group to note all that is said about darkness and light as the passage is being read.

Talk about what Jesus is saying about himself and what he says about the darkness of the Pharisees. Discuss how you talk about 'darkness' and 'sin' to the children today, reminding them to be careful what vocabulary they use and how it is expressed. Pray for each other in small groups, that you will be able to share with the children how great Jesus is and how he has come to turn darkness into light, to bring his light into our lives and give us life.

CLEARING THE GROUND
10 minutes

Play some lively music and display the **Wastewatchers** logo to welcome the children as they arrive and are registered. The children are given their badge for the day and go to their Taskforce Groups. This is an opportunity for Taskforce Leaders to get to review what the children think of the club so far, especially the Bible stories and what they have found out in the Bible discovery sections. Can anyone remember the *Learn and remember verse*(s)? Make any new children especially welcome.

Taskforce Groups

What you need

- More junk for your model, sticky tape, scissors or
- Felt-tip pens and the giant rubbish picture (page 54)

What you do

Each group should spend time together on their giant rubbish picture or on creating their junk model. Any children who have brought jokes, pictures or questions should drop them in the bottle bank.

ON THE TIP
35 minutes

The Binmen/women welcome the children to **Wastewatchers**, especially any new children.

Warm up

What you need

- Energetic music and a plan of movements for the children to follow

What you do

Lead a workout to music with a strong beat. The purpose of this is to let the children have fun and use up some energy. As they sit down, ask them what they notice about the tip, especially any comments on the pond.

Wastewatchers challenge

Everyone is involved in this challenge.

What you need

- Ten short recorded sounds of noises heard at night, eg wind, owl, dog/fox, footsteps, voices, cat, car engine, mouse, aeroplane, slamming car door, rain, ticking clock

What you do

In their Taskforce Groups, ask the children to imagine they are in bed at night and to close their eyes. Here are ten sounds they might hear. In their groups, can they identify the sounds

so that their Taskforce Leader can record the answers? Be aware of any children who have hearing difficulties and may find this challenge demanding. Maybe they can help switch the sounds on and off. Children of all ages should be able to do this equally well.

Play the sounds once, allowing time for a discussion of the answer in groups. Then play them again checking who has got the right answers. Talk about what it is about the dark that we may not like.

Alternatively, ask one person from each group to come to the front to be blindfolded and led through a series of obstacles, or asked to do something that is hard to do if you are blindfolded. For ideas of blindfold games see *Everyone's a Winner,* Ruth Wills, Scripture Union, 2001.

Songs

Sing the **Wastewatchers** song as a round if you are confident of this. Also sing other non-confessional songs that are suitable to use with children who know little about Jesus.

> In the trial, the children loved the 'What a load of rubbish' beginning and managed the round surprisingly easily.

Tell the story

Show Episode 3 of the DVD, in which Jesus gives the blind man his sight but does more than that, shining his light into the man's life and giving him life. This contrasts with the attitudes of the Pharisees who remain in their darkness.

Alternatively, tell the story in John 9:1–41 in the following way. The repeated phrase is 'Everyone, except Jesus!' but you will need to use your own words in the retelling.

One of the leaders dresses up as a cleaner in the temple, someone who sweeps the courtyard. He begins by introducing himself as Daniel. He talks about the Pharisees, who are very serious and very clever and very good. They are the men who teach people about how they should live a good life. Everyone listens to them when they talk and never questions what they say. Everyone, except Jesus!

He explains what happened when Jesus healed the blind man, on a Saturday, the day when everyone has a rest from work. Surely he knew that healing someone on a work day was against the rules! Everyone knew that. Everyone, except Jesus!

The teachers and leaders interviewed this blind man, who could now see, to find out what had happened. Had he really been blind? Was he not fooling everyone? They even interviewed his parents who said he had been born blind but they didn't know how he had come to see. In fact, the parents did not really seem to be on the side of this man, their son. The teachers threw the man out of the temple. Everyone seemed to be against him. Everyone, except Jesus!

But the blind man (who wasn't blind any more) knew that Jesus was someone special. He knew he had been healed and that it was a miracle. He knew that the way the Pharisees were treating him was wrong. They were meant to be so good but inside they were anything but that. But everyone seemed to think they were always right. Everyone, except Jesus!

Jesus came to find the man. The man realised Jesus had come from God and he put his trust in Jesus. That meant that he had the light of Jesus inside him. The Pharisees couldn't see their need to put their trust in Jesus so it was as if they were blind. But anyone who puts their trust in Jesus has his light inside.

Explanation

Either the binmen or the storyteller need to explain the two clear points to this story. You may want to do this if you have watched the DVD. Practice how to explain this to the children by talking this over with a couple of other leaders.

The blind man was changed from not being able to see, to seeing everything. Just imagine how different his life would be? Ask the children what he could now do.

But he was changed in another way. Jesus had come to shine his light on things that are wrong in the world.

a) Things that are wrong in the world around us.

We have seen how all sorts of things in the world around us are all messed up. Do you remember what had gone wrong in the garden in the story on Day 1? (People had decided not to do what God wanted. They began to fall out. They found it very hard work to look after the animals and to dig the earth to grow vegetables. They began to feel pain. People thought they knew better than God. That's when things went wrong. And ever since then, people have not always pleased God and there has been trouble in the world.)

In our Taskforce Project, we are trying to change things and make them better. If you have already started the project, talk about what has happened – or talk about what you plan to do.

b) Things that are wrong in each of us.

But it is not just things that are wrong in the world around us. There are also things that are wrong in each of us too. We fall out with people. We do what we want when we know we shouldn't. We don't always tell the truth. Jesus showed the man that inside him there was darkness too. Jesus said that he came to judge the world, to show people where they had not done what pleases God. The Bible calls that 'sin'. Jesus had come to shine his light to show people that they had not done what pleases God.

He also came to take away the darkness and put his light there instead, to give life where before there was darkness.

The Pharisees however, were not living in a way that pleased God. But they thought they were just fine! They were so blind that they refused to listen to what Jesus said about them needing his light.

Find the WasteWatcherWord (WWW)

From darkness into light

What you need
- 21 tea lights and a lighter/matches
- A whiteboard or large sheet of paper with dashes for the 21 letters

What you do
Invite the children to call out a letter at a time. Every letter that is in the WWW is written on the appropriate dash – you will need two goes for I, N, O, R, S and T. Explain that there are six letters that come twice. Which ones are they? For every correct letter light a candle until they are all lit.

Pray for the world

Light a candle and explain that you are doing that as a reminder that Jesus, the light for the world, is with you now to hear you when you talk with him.

Either pray simply for anything or anyone the children have asked to pray about, or describe one situation in the world that could be described as dark, such as a war zone or a natural disaster. Ask God to bring his light there, to end violence and suffering.

TASKFORCE
50 minutes

Refreshments

5 minutes
Serve the children some refreshments in small groups.

Bible discovery

15 minutes

With older children

If you are using *Little Green Pages* turn to page 30–33, or have enough copies of John 9:1–41 for each child. You will need some brown-coloured flour and water paste and a blown-up balloon with a face drawn on it, which has just the shape of the eyes without an iris. As the story is read (you could do this in a narrative way), put the brown paste on the eyes of the balloon face and then wash it off! With a felt-tip add the irises to the eyes and eyelashes to make them look more seeing! You could use proper mud or clay!

Then look up the following verses and write down what people said about Jesus. You could do this together using page 33 of the booklet. If you are not using the booklet, divide a sheet of paper in two columns, labelled 'What the Pharisees said' and 'What the man said about Jesus'.

Verse 16: This man doesn't come from God (Pharisees)
Verse 17: He is a prophet (man)
Verse 24: He is a sinner (Pharisees)
Verse 33: Jesus came from God (man) (You may need to explain that 'Son of Man' was a name that Jesus sometimes called himself.)

What did Jesus say he had come to do? You could put this into a code for the children to work out.
Verse 5: Jesus said, 'While I am in the world, I am light for the world.'
Verse 39: Jesus said, 'I came to judge the people of this world.'

With younger children

Read the story out loud using the mud as with the older children.

Jesus was really pleased that the man could see and he went to find him after everyone else had left him on his own. The man was really pleased to be with Jesus and so grateful. Jesus knew that this man wanted to trust him. This meant that the man was not dark inside – unlike the Pharisees. Talk about what that means to you that you have Jesus' light inside you and know that Jesus is with you. Complete the Eco Sheet together.

For all children

Explore the story by adapting the questions below to suit your group:
- Can you imagine what it is like to be blind?
- Was the reason why this man was blind because he had done wrong or his parents had done wrong or neither? Explore the reasons why people cannot see.
- The Pharisees were not at all happy that the blind man could see because they did not like Jesus. Why was this? Why do you think people did not like someone like Jesus who was so good and kind?
- The Pharisees or teachers of the law could all see, but Jesus said they were blind. What did he mean? What does it mean to be blind or dark inside? (Expect all sorts of answers and be ready to talk about what it means to you to have Jesus' light inside you.)

Help the children identify something they think is bad or dark and a situation where they want to see Jesus shining his light. Some children will have latched on to the idea of darkness inside them, others will be thinking of places where there is a war or incidents such as bullying in the playground. Ask Jesus to shine his light there.

'We thank you Jesus that you are the light for the world. We pray that you will shine your light in _____ (ask the children to speak out their 'places'). We pray that you will shine your light in us too. Amen.'

Games

15 minutes
The theme of all these games is that of light and sources of light. Each game reminds the children of the story for today.

Post-a-light

What you need

- Paper squares with images of sources of light – for example sun, moon, torch, light bulb, candle, lantern (one of each image for the containers and at least ten squares, with a mix of images for every child in the game)
- Six containers, each marked with one source of light
- One bag per team to hold squares
- Stopwatch

What you do

Place the containers all over the room. Place each team's squares in a different bag. Give the children five minutes to post as many of their squares in the correct containers, one at a time. In turn, each team member pulls out a square and runs to post it in the right box. You could mark the team's colour or symbol on the back and at the end count which team has posted the most. Older children will do this more quickly and easily than younger ones so either have mixed teams or limit the age band playing this game at any one time.

Freeze in the light

What you need

• Music (live or recorded)
• Darkened room (check that the children are comfortable being in a darkened room)
• Torch

What you do

This is like musical chairs, except when the light goes out, everyone freezes. The music plays all the time just to fill the 'sound space'. A leader (or two) goes round shining their torch and anyone who moves has to sit out.

Light circle

Sit all the children in a circle and give each child the name of one of these six sources of light, one after the other: candle, torch, sun, moon, lantern, light bulb. If you have played Post-a-light the children will be aware of these light sources. When you call out one of the names, all the children with that name, run round in a clock-wise direction. The last one to sit down has to put their hand on their head and keep it there for the rest of the game. If this happens to a child a second time, they put both hands on their head. A third time they have to hop! (But they do not have to sit out!) When you shout 'Dark into Light' all the children run round.

Photos

Older children might enjoy taking photos with a digital camera, which will involve a flash and then arranging the photos as a collage. Photos could either be of the club or of sources of light that you have collected beforehand. If you have anyone who has expertise in photography that involves a darkroom, children would be fascinated to develop their own pictures from negatives. You could only do this with a small group and would need to ensure you had enough time. Also be aware of child protection issues! Working with a small group of children doing photography gives plenty of opportunity to talk and build relationships.

Crafts

15 minutes

Stained glass

Here are two ways to create 'stained glass'.

What you need

• Glass paints and outliner (available from craft shops)
• Either small jars/tea light holders and tea lights or sheets of acetate

What you do

If you are using jars or tea light holders, show the children how to use the outliner to draw a design on the glass. When this has dried, the children can paint different colours in the outline. You may have to let one side dry before the children turn the jar/holder round to paint the other side. When the jar/holder is dry, place a tea light inside. Make sure the children know that these should only be lit in the presence of an adult.

If you are using acetates, show the children how to draw a design on the acetate and then colour in the design with the paint. When the paint is dry, the children can stick the acetate in the window to let the light shine through. (You may need to use a particular kind of acetate – check the packaging of the glass paint.) You could also make a frame for the acetate.

Other craft suggestions

• Make a candle holder from clay.
• Lamp shade – design and make a lamp shade especially if it's to be used with a low-wattage, energy-saving bulb. This would be suitable for older children and might take more than one day. They could only or mainly use recyclable materials. Alternatively, they could create a large paper lantern.
• Invisible writing paintings – using candle wax, draw a picture or message, then paint over it to reveal the 'invisible' picture/message.
• An open and shut eye – create and cut out on card a scene from the story within an eye shape. The children colour or paint this. Cut out a closed eye shape and attach the latter to the eye picture with a split pin in the corner.

Be aware of safety issues for each of these activities.

 **BIG CLEAN UP**
30 minutes

Bottle bank

Sing one or two songs as the children arrive and read out any suitable jokes, display pictures and answer any insightful questions from the bottle bank.

Quiz

Keep this short, to remind everyone of the story. Score by giving each child who answers correctly a small unlit candle.

For example:

Q How long had the man been blind?
A All his life.
Q How did Jesus heal the man?
A By smearing mud on his eyes.)
Q Why were the Pharisees cross?
A Because Jesus said they were blind.
Q What did the Pharisees do to the man?
A They threw him out of the temple.
Q When the man realised it was Jesus who had healed him, what did he do?
A Worshipped him.
Q What is today's WWW?
A From darkness to light.

Drama

The park keeper leads in the three blindfolded teenagers, because he wants to surprise them with the pond. Barry, being blindfolded, gets in the way and sits on some wet paint. This emphasises the difficulty of not being able to see.

This happened to me…

Invite a team member to be interviewed or to share the story of how they came to know that there was darkness inside them, but Jesus' light shone on them. They should also talk about how he helps them to have a close relationship with God. Begin the interview by asking them what they are afraid of in the dark and more generally what they are afraid of, to demonstrate to the children how normal they are. At the end ask them what they like best about today's story. Make sure that what they say about Jesus is simple, in child-friendly language and uses the phrases about sin and light and being out of relationship with God that you have been using all this session. Read pages 30–31 for more suggestions.

Learn and remember

Today's memory verse is a continuation of John 8:12: Jesus said, 'I am the light for the world! Follow me and you won't be walking in the dark…' Sing the song together. If you are having a different memory verse each day, learn all or part of this verse. Just remind the children how the Pharisees were walking in the dark, refusing to come to Jesus' light.

Light experiment

Remind children of the aim of the experiment and see if there is any difference yet between the two plants that are not in the dark.

Creative prayer idea

What you need

- a candle placed inside a stable container for each Taskforce Group
- a lighter

What you do

Sit the children in a circle in their Taskforce Groups. Ask the children to be very quiet and ask them to think of something in their life that they know they do which does not please God. Remind them that this is darkness, inside them. Remind them that Jesus came to shine his light into dark places. Nothing is hidden from him. He is the light for the world.

Light the candles and then thank Jesus that he shows us what we have done wrong and then forgives us. Ask each child to talk to God (in their head) about what they have done wrong and, if they are sorry about it, ask him to forgive them. Pray a simple prayer to conclude this time. Make sure the candles are blown out before anyone moves back to their Taskforce Group area.

TASKFORCE TOO
5 minutes

Spend the last five minutes of the club in Taskforce Groups, finishing off any craft or puzzles from *Little Green Pages*. Taskforce Leaders should take this opportunity to chat about the day's Bible story, asking the children what they found out, as well as asking them what they thought.

Taskforce Leaders should also make sure they know how each child is getting home. As each child is leaving, they should say goodbye and remind them about the next session.

FINAL CLEAR UP

After the children have left and the clear-up is over, gather the team together for a time of reflection, comment and prayer. You may wish to use the evaluation form on page 50.

Suggestions for a suitable family and community event to accompany this session are on pages 34–36. Showing a film or organising a trip out to a local nature reserve, wildlife park or swimming pool would be obvious activities to offer.

From darkness to light

eco sheet

3

Jesus shone his light in this world to show up wrong things. Write or draw in the teardrop something that you think is bad or dark.

Write or draw in the light bulb a place or situation where you want Jesus to shine his light. Ask Jesus to shine his light in this place and in you too.

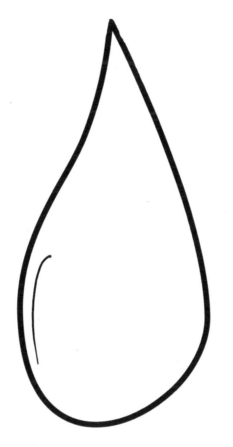

The blind man had difficulty seeing anything, until Jesus healed him. Use your eyes to see how many eyes are hidden in this picture.

"Jesus said, 'I am the light for the world! Follow me and you won't be walking in the dark. You will have the light that gives life.'" John 8:12

From death to life

DAY 4

AIMS FOR TODAY

To help the children understand what they are hearing about Jesus' desire to change them and the world around us.

God's Word

- To hear about Jesus' death and his rejection by those who chose to walk in the dark.
- To discover that Jesus' death was planned. He came to be lifted up on the cross, just like the snake was lifted up in the desert (John 3:13–21), and he came alive!

Word for us

To recognise that because of his death, Jesus fulfilled what he had planned to do. He shines in the darkness, shows up sin for what it is and gives life, both now and for ever, as the *Learn and remember verse* reminds us.

Bible story

Jesus was judged and rejected but came alive again (selected verses from John 19,20). John 3:13–21 is also essential background to understanding the importance the writer of John's Gospel places upon the cross.

Key word from John 1:

'He came into his own world, but his own nation did not welcome him' (John 1:11).

The emphasis of this session is on Jesus' death. We need to show the children that Jesus knew he was going to die, to be lifted up on the cross. All who look to him, aware of the darkness, will be coming to the light and will receive life. Jesus shows up the darkness of sin and gives true life! There may be some children who want to make a commitment to follow Jesus today.

The world of a child

The story of Jesus' death and resurrection is not well known. Most adults do not know why Christians celebrate Easter, so children are even less likely to know. Jesus' death can appear as a failure, he didn't manage to do what he appeared to set out to do. It is important that we stress that this was all part of God's plan. Jesus did achieve what he came to do. He came to die in order to make it possible for all people to know God, to have life for ever. Do not dwell on the gory bits of the crucifixion but make it clear that he really did die. The story of the cross is a mystery so even if the children only understand a little more, we should be satisfied. Some children may not come back for the triumphant ending, which will be the focus of the final session, so make sure that everyone knows that Jesus came alive again.

The light experiment by this stage may be working which is a clear illustration of how light gives life. The children will remember this.

Consider how you will enable children to make an appropriate response to Jesus. Use the words 'Follow Jesus' since they are the ones in the *Learn and remember verse*. For information about commitment booklets for children of all ages, turn to the inside front cover.

GETTING READY

Rubbish tip

The tip is even smaller, with a bench and pond from previous days. A pile of branches is needed today to build a trellis. You will need two long branches or planks.

Physical preparation

Talk through the session's programme, and make sure that everyone is aware of their responsibilities. Encourage the team to be as welcoming and interactive with the children as possible. Ask Taskforce Leaders to make sure that they speak some encouraging words to every child in their group. Ensure that all the resources are ready for the various activities.

Equipment checklist – Day 4

Security: registration forms, badges, pens, team lists

Binmen/women: running order, notes, as many cross shapes as you can make for **Wastewatchers** challenge, resources for WWW, **Wastewatchers** DVD, plants from light experiment

Storyteller: resources

Taskforce Groups: resources for CLEARING THE GROUND, pens, Bibles, *Little Green Pages* or Eco Sheets, Bible discovery notes

Creative prayer: resources

Music: music for your chosen songs, including the **Wastewatchers** song, *Learn and remember verse* song, other background music

Drama: props

Technology: check PA, OHP/data projector and DVD player are all working and in focus

Games and craft: all the resources for your chosen activities

Refreshments: drinks and biscuits, or other snacks

Rubbish tip: a pile of branches and two long branches or planks

Spiritual preparation

Begin by singing a song known to you all about the cross eg 'On the cross', 'When I survey' or 'The cross has said it all'.

Together read John 19:17–30. How did Jesus show that even though he may have appeared powerless, he was still in control? What does that say about him?

Then read Numbers 21:4–9 to remind people of the story which is the background to John 3:13–21. Jesus knew he was going to die.
Today you are going to talk about Jesus' death which was all part of God's plan. Why does it matter that his death was planned? How will you explain these verses to the children? John 1:11 sums it up well. (Check how team members are getting on with the challenge of learning John 1:1–14!)

How are you going to talk about John 8:12? Jesus' purpose was to make it possible that we no longer walk in the dark (what does that mean?) and that we have the light that gives life. (What sort of life are we talking about?)
In small groups, pray for each other and the children by name. The fourth day is often the most demanding because children are familiar with the club, some may be tired and the message of the cross is so important that frequently leaders of holiday clubs report that they are aware of a real spiritual battle. As overall leader, pray for God's protection on all of you. You could read Colossians 2:13–15 to focus your minds!

CLEARING THE GROUND
10 minutes

Play some lively music and display the **Wastewatchers** logo to welcome the children as they arrive and are registered. The children are given their badge for the day and go to their Taskforce Groups. This is an opportunity for Taskforce Leaders to get to review what the children think of the club so far, especially the Bible stories and what they have found out in the Bible discovery sections. Can anyone remember the *Learn and remember verse*(s)? Make any new children especially welcome.

Taskforce Groups

What you need

- More junk for your model, sticky tape, scissors or
- Felt-tip pens and the giant rubbish picture (page 54)

This time is an opportunity for Taskforce Leaders to get to know the children better and find out what they enjoyed yesterday. Each group should spend time together on their giant rubbish picture or on creating their junk model rubbish tip. Any children who have brought jokes, pictures or questions should drop them in the bottle bank.

ON THE TIP
35 minutes

The Binmen/women welcome the children to **Wastewatchers**.

Warm up

What you need

- Energetic music and a plan of movements for the children to follow

What you do

Lead a workout to music with a strong beat. The purpose of this is to let the children have fun and use up some energy. As they sit down, ask them what they notice about the tip, especially any comments on the planks and branches.

Wastewatcher challenge

Everyone is involved in this challenge.

What you need

- As many cross shapes as you can hide around the building

What you do

In Taskforce Groups, the children identify as many cross shapes that they can in one minute. Remind them that some cross shapes are part of the building, such as window frames, crosses on pictures or carvings. If you are not free to move around because there are too many children, put the crosses so that children can see them from where they are sitting. Cross badges or earrings count too! Altogether share and count what the groups have seen.

Songs

Sing the **Wastewatchers** song and other non-confessional songs, suitable to use with children who know little about Jesus.

Learn and remember

If you want a new memory verse for today, John 3:16 would be an excellent one. Or if you are using the single verse, finish learning John 8:12: 'Jesus said, "I am the light for the world! Follow me and you won't be walking in the dark. You will have the light that gives life."' John 8:12.
It is worth finishing this today since some children may not come on the final day.
Talk about the life that Jesus, the light for the world, can give. What does it mean to follow Jesus?

Light experiment

So is the light having an effect? Make the link with the *Learn and remember verse*. You could give the children a peak at the plant in the dark.

Tell the story

Show the DVD Episode 4 – the people who hate Jesus put him to death. But he shows that he is still in control. His resurrection is hinted at. You may find it helpful to explain the story of Moses and the snake and the similarity between that story and Jesus' story after you have watched the DVD.

Alternatively, tell the story from John 19 in the following way:

What you need

- A box of junk, including some old rope, a hammer and one big nail, a cross shape, some white cloth, a toy snake, a pole and any other props to help tell the story
- A prop from the three previous days

> In the trial, these objects were wheeled in on a wheelbarrow – this really kept the children's interest.

Explain that in your box/wheelbarrow you have a number of things, some of them you might find on a rubbish tip. Begin by bringing out the reminders from previous days.

(*Bring out the reminder of Day 1.*) Remember that we discovered what a wonderful world God had made, but things began to go wrong.

(*Bring out the reminder of Day 2.*) Remember how Jesus came to the rescue when things went wrong at a wedding? What did he do?

(*Bring out the reminder of Day 3.*) Jesus healed a blind man. What did the enemies of Jesus say about this? They were living in darkness, without the light of Jesus.

Jesus could do great things no one else could do because he was God himself. But more and more people did not like what he said. He told them that people who did not listen to God or who refused to live in a way that pleased God were living in the dark. Maybe they were hurting others, telling lies or being selfish or cruel.

Jesus' light showed up these wrong things and that made people uncomfortable.

Jesus' enemies laid a plot. At the dead of night, they arranged for soldiers to arrest Jesus, tie him up as a prisoner and take him away to appear before a judge. (*Bring out the rope.*) It was not a fair trial because people told lies about Jesus. They said he had done some dreadful things, which was just not true! All this happened very quickly, in the middle of the night. No one spoke up for Jesus.

It was still early in the morning when a crowd of people gathered outside the building where the judge was. Jesus was made to stand outside where everyone could see him and the judge asked the crowd what should happen to Jesus. And do you know what the crowd shouted? They yelled, 'Nail Jesus to a cross! Kill him!' These were the people who only a few weeks before had queued up to listen to Jesus and see what he was doing.

So Jesus was taken to a hill outside of the city. Soldiers nailed him to a cross which was lifted up high so that everyone could see him. (*Bring out the nail, hammer and the cross shape.*) Jesus was left to die, like a criminal. But even as he was dying, Jesus thought of other people. He saw his mother there. He told one of his best friends to look after his mother as though she was his own mother.

But was it all a terrible mistake? No! Do you know what Jesus said just before he died? He said, 'Everything is done!' He knew that it was in God's plan that he should die. He had completed the job God had given him to do. In fact, he had known for a long time that this was what would happen.

You see, he had once reminded a teacher called Nicodemus about something that happened to God's people when they had been living in

the desert, long ago. They had disobeyed God, so God punished them by sending lots of poisonous snakes. People began to die from the snake bites. Some of them were sorry because of the wrong they had done and they asked Moses, their leader, to ask God to rescue them and take away the snakes.

God told Moses to carve a snake out of bronze and stick it on a tall pole. (*Show the snake and pole.*) He then told the people that anyone who got bitten had only to look at the snake and they would live and be OK. And that's what happened. People who believed what Moses said looked at the bronze snake and they were cured. People who did not believe what Moses said did not look – and they died.

Jesus predicted that he was going to be lifted up for everyone to see him. Whoever looked to him and was sorry for how they had wronged God would have life. If they had faith in Jesus and let his light shine on them, they would live. If they did not look to Jesus, they would not have life.

We are not talking about looking with our eyes because not that many people could see Jesus when he died on the cross. Instead we are talking about 'looking' like we might trust someone. For example, you might be out of your depth in the swimming pool and in trouble. The lifesaver doesn't ask you actually to look at them, simply to trust them to rescue you.

(*Bring out the cloth.*) Jesus' body was taken down from the cross, wrapped in white cloth and put in a cold, stone cave. Three days later Jesus came alive again. Yes! He showed that his enemies had not won! The light had triumphed over the darkness. He had new life and he could now give new life to anyone who followed him.

We'll find out more about Jesus coming alive again next time!

Find the WasteWatcherWord (WWW)

From death to life

What you need

- Seven long strips of paper with sticky backing/Blu-tack
- Six short strips and one that bends to make the curve of a D, also with sticky backing
- A board to stick the letters on

What you do

In this activity, you are going to create the WWW from strips of paper (You will need to practise how this works so you can help the children if they can't do it.)

First, create the word DEATH on the board. Explain that you have five instructions to transform the word DEATH into another word. Ask for two volunteers and give them the following instructions:

- Get rid of the first letter.

- The first letter of the old word now becomes the last letter of the new word. (Move 'E' to the end of the word – you will then have 'ATHE'.)

- The last letter of the old word becomes the first of the new word. (Move 'H' to the beginning to make 'HATE'. Ask the children if this is the end. No! Jesus came to defeat death and hate.) It loses its right post and drops its middle. (The 'H' then becomes 'L' to make 'LATE'.)

- The letter you drink ('T') becomes the second letter of the new word ('LTAE') but loses its lid (LIAE).

- The only letter left is now the third letter of the new word. But its left post stands up straight, and its right post becomes a lid ('F', so the word becomes 'LIFE').

DEATH has become LIFE, FROM DEATH TO LIFE!

Pray for the world

Write down a list of all the people the children and leaders have asked to be prayed for, so that everyone can see it. Explain a little about each person, as appropriate. Ask the children to choose one person and then ask them to close their eyes and just talk to Jesus about that person.

Alternatively, you could pray for the teachers at the schools the children go to and especially for any children who are about to change schools or are facing big decisions about schools.

 **TASKFORCE**
50 minutes

Refreshments

5 minutes

Serve the children some refreshments in small groups.

Bible discovery

15 minutes

With older children

If you are using *Little Green Pages* turn to page 36, or have enough copies of John 19:25–30 and John 3:13–15,19–21 for each child. Sit the children in a circle and ask them to underline all the words Jesus said when he was on the cross. Explore the story adapting the questions below. Then turn to page 24 in *LIttle Green Pages* to see what Jesus said about his death in John 3:13–15 and the story which can be found in Numbers 21:4–9. Finally, do the puzzle on page 37. If time, you could take the story on to John 20:1–10 to clarify that Jesus' death was not an accident and was not the end either. He came alive again! He was transformed!

With younger children

Read out loud John 19:25–30 (you could miss out the names of the other women). Remind them that this is very sad but it was not the end because Jesus came alive again. Then

read them the story from Numbers 21:4-9. Just as people had to look to the bronze snake to be cured and to live, so people need to look to Jesus to let his light give them life. Explain what 'looking' means for children who might think it literally means they have to look at Jesus. Talk about the light experiment to show how light is needed to keep things alive and growing. Complete the Eco Sheets after that.

With all children

Explore the story by adapting the questions below to suit your group:

- Even though Jesus was in awful pain, how did he go on showing his love for other people?

- What do you think Jesus meant when he said, "Everything is done!"?

- What had Jesus come to do? Turn to pages 24–25 in *Little Green Pages* and read John 3:13–15. Ask the children what they remember about the story of the bronze snake in the desert. Then ask them to put a sparkle around the word 'light' and a dark cloud around the word 'dark' or 'evil' in John 3:19–21.

- Remind the children of the *Learn and remember verse* and see if they can remember the two parts of yesterday's story: Jesus has come to shine his light to show where there is darkness and sin; Jesus came to shine his light that gives life, which was what he gave the blind man.

- Talk about what Jesus' death means to you and what it means to you that his light has given you life – both real life now and the promise of life with God forever!

- Thank Jesus that his death was planned and that he came to shine light where there is darkness and to give new life to everyone who looks to him and believes him.

Games

15 minutes

The theme of all these games is crosses, which is only a tenuous link with the theme of this session. But they are energetic games and will allow the children to let off steam, which may be needed after the challenge of the earlier part of the session.

Diagonal races

What you need

A large room with teams in each corner

What you do

Play a series of races where some children are positioned at point A and some at point B (see diagram below). Each moves straight ahead so that their paths cross in the centre. Point out the shape they are making. Suitable races might be hopping, bouncing a ball, three-legged races, wheelbarrow races and egg and spoon. Avoid running races since that will result in collisions.

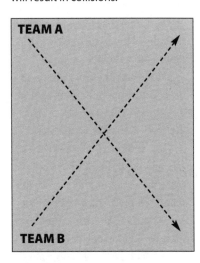

TEAM A

TEAM B

Handball – the noughts against the crosses

What you need

A ball, two goals

What you do

Split the children into two teams. Appoint a goalkeeper for each team. Children need to pat the ball along the ground with one hand, the other being behind their back.
Or a variation of this game!

Knotty problem

Everyone stands in a circle holding hands and then step over arms and

climb through legs to get knotted up, without breaking the circle. Someone tries to disentangle the circle. What a mess but in the same way, Jesus came to sort out the knottiness in life.

Obedience games

Simon says, "Captain's on board" etc where children have to do what they are told at the right time and in the right way. Point out that Jesus obeyed God and did the right thing, at the right time, in the right way.
(This last game reinforces Jesus' obedience.)

Craft

15 minutes

Talk with the children about the story of Jesus' death as you make these cross-shaped crafts.

Cross-stitch

What you need

- Cross-stitch equipment (needles, base, different coloured thread)
- Pattern (see **Wastewatchers** website for this and for more advice on cross-stitch)

What you need

Cross-stitch is something that many children enjoy. Use a pattern of your own design (there may be someone in your church who can create this for you). Make sure they have plenty of colours. It is a good idea to thread needles beforehand with younger children!

Mexican star cross

What you need

- Two drinking straws, kebab sticks or pieces of dowelling per child
- Sticky tape
- Different coloured wool or string
- Diagram from **Wastewatchers** website

What you do

Show the children how to make the diamond pattern below before they start. Hold the end of the wool at the centre of the cross, pass the other end

over one arm of the cross, round the back and onto the next arm, pulling the yarn fairly tight. Continue round the cross changing colours as you go. Tie the end of one colour to the start of the next.

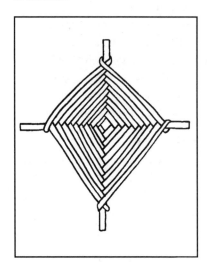

Other craft ideas

- Make a Hama-bead coaster with a cross-shaped pattern. Find time to iron the beads during the session or make sure each child's beads are labelled and kept safe so that you can do the ironing later without losing any beads!
- Make stained glass windows with a cross-shape (see page 77 for more detailed instructions).

BIG CLEAN UP

30 minutes

Bottle bank

Sing one or two songs as the children arrive and read out any suitable jokes, display pictures and answer any questions from the bottle bank.

Drama

The area around the bench is now tidy but there is a pile of branches on one side of the stage. The characters decide to make a trellis. Much slapstick ensues as they attempt to make the trellis and then they all fall out! But then they realise that they need to change.

Quiz

Keep this short, to remind everyone of the story. Score by playing a game of noughts and crosses – one team is noughts, the other crosses. When they get a question right, they should decide where they want to go on a noughts and crosses board. Make sure that answers can be known from what has been spoken about in this session, so as not to disadvantage children who do not know much about Jesus.

For example:

Why did Jesus' enemies dislike him?
What time of day was Jesus arrested?
Where was he taken?
What time of day was he brought out in front of the crowd?
What did the crowd shout?
What have you just read that Jesus said when he was on the cross? (Three possible answers.)
What is today's WWW? (From death to life.)

This happened to me…

Invite a team member to be interviewed or to share their story of why Jesus' death is important to them and is not an accident. What does it mean to them to follow Jesus and have his light that gives life? They could talk about how they have 'looked' to Jesus and been given life. At the end, ask them what they like best about today's story. Make sure that what they say about Jesus is simple, in child-friendly language and uses the phrases about being in a relationship with God that you have been using all this session. Read pages 30–31 for more suggestions.

Creative prayer idea

What you do

Ask the children to copy these actions as you pray. The first time through, a couple of leaders could show how it is done. Say this prayer together twice:

Jesus, we know your death was very painful. (*Point to the centre of the palm on both hands.*)
Thank you that you died on the cross for us. (*Make a cross shape with hands.*)
Thank you that you died because you love us. (*Make an X – a kiss not a wrong – with hands.*)
Thank you that you came alive again. (*Jump up from the floor joyfully.*)
And that means you are with us now. (*Stretch out arms in a welcome.*)
Hooray! (*Wave arms in the air.*)

TASKFORCE TOO

5 minutes

Spend the last five minutes of the club in Taskforce Groups, finishing off any craft or puzzles from *Little Green Pages*. Taskforce Leaders should take this opportunity to chat about the day's Bible story, asking the children what they found out, as well as asking them what they thought.
Taskforce Leaders should also make sure they know how each child is getting home. As each child is leaving, they should say goodbye and remind them about the next session.

FINAL CLEAR UP

After the children have left and the clear-up is over, gather the team together for a time of reflection, comment and prayer. You may wish to use the evaluation form on page 50.

Suggestions for family and community events to follow up this session are on pages 34–36. It would be appropriate to run a parents' evening with suitable babysitting services on offer at this later stage in the week. Issues that parents are interested in such as choosing schools, discipline and coping with change are all possible topics.

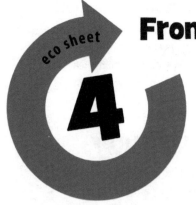

From death to life

"Jesus said, 'Everything is done!' He bowed his head and died."
(John 19:30)

Jesus died. But his death was planned. Jesus knew he was going to be lifted up on the cross, so that anyone who looked to him and believed would have life. Find these words in the wordsearch. The leftover letters tell you what happened three days later.

w	d	e	s	a
i	t	h	k	j
n	l	i	u	e
e	f	e	l	s
n	a	i	l	u
c	r	o	s	s

CROSS JESUS NAIL SKULL WINE

From _ _ _ _ _ to _ _ _ _

Jesus came alive again to show that his death was part of God's plan.

He came to shine his light in the darkness.

He came to give life to everyone who follows him.

Colour in this banner.

Thank you Jesus that you died to give us the light that gives life.

From sadness to joy

AIMS FOR TODAY

To conclude the holiday club, reviewing all that has happened and been taught. Ensure that every child and their carer knows what else is planned for the coming months. Give children an appropriate opportunity to respond to Jesus.

God's Word
• To rediscover that Jesus died but he came alive again and is alive today!

Word for us
• To rejoice that Jesus is with us, wants to forgive us and take away the darkness so we can have a lifelong relationship with him. We need to make a response.

Bible story:
Jesus' resurrection (John 20:11–18).

Key word from John 1
'We saw his true glory, the glory of the only Son of the Father. From him all the kindness and all the truth of God have come down to us' (John 1:14b).
We celebrate that Jesus is alive. Our sadness can be turned to joy! (Have the team learnt John 1:1–14 by now?)

The world of a child
The story of Jesus' resurrection is a mystery. How can someone who died come alive again? But for children there are all sorts of 'wondering' questions: what sort of body did he have? Did he look the same? So when did he die after that? Where is he now if he isn't dead? How can Jesus be with us if I can't see him? Questions about what happens when we die and where grandma is are also likely. Prepare by thinking as a team of all the questions that might be asked and thinking how you would best answer them.

The language we use is important. Consider how you will enable children to make an appropriate response to Jesus and what you will say or give to their parents or carers. For information about commitment booklets for children of all ages, turn to the inside front cover. As a team you could work through these booklets.

GETTING READY

Rubbish tip
Today you should have your beautiful park, although the props for the drama remind everyone that this is still a tip (just about!). Use your imagination to make this as attractive as possible. You might even want to ask someone to bring an unusual pet – that will certainly interest the children! It is important that the tip is now environmentally friendly and a place of pleasure. It has been transformed!
As this is the last session, try to generate a party atmosphere in your venue. There needs to be lots of joy in evidence!

Physical preparation
Talk through the session's programme, and make sure that everyone is aware of their responsibilities. Encourage the team to be as welcoming and interactive with the children as possible. Ask Taskforce Leaders to make sure that they speak some encouraging words to every child in their group. Ensure that all the resources are ready for the various activities.

Equipment checklist – Day 5
Security: registration forms, badges, pens, team lists
Binmen/women: running order, notes, make-up and remover, together with hair bands and ribbons for **Wastewatchers** challenge, resources for WWW, Wastewatchers DVD, plants from light experiment

Storyteller: resources
Taskforce Groups: resources for CLEARING THE GROUND, pens, Bibles, *Little Green Pages* or Eco Sheets, Bible discovery resources, Bible discovery notes
Creative prayer: resources
Music: music for your chosen songs, including the **Wastewatchers** song, *Learn and remember verse* song, other background music
Drama: props
Technology: check PA, OHP/data projector and DVD player are all working and in focus
Games and craft: all the resources for your chosen activities
Refreshments: drinks and biscuits, or other snacks
Rubbish tip: junk turned into useful things, eg tyres turned into plant pot holders

Spiritual preparation

Begin by writing up all the things to be thankful for from **Wastewatchers**. Sing a couple of songs that are praise offerings to God.

Read John 20:1–18, asking everyone to decide at what point Mary experienced various changes of mood. Discuss this in small groups. Mary was one of the first to see the risen Jesus in all his glory! Turn back to John 1:14 and, in the groups, ask people to put this verse in their own words, as you think especially about the wonder of the resurrection.

Pray for one another as you bring the great news of Jesus, alive and with us, to the children today. Do emphasise that each child and parent/carer needs to know about the plans for the following weeks.

CLEARING THE GROUND
10 minutes

Play some lively music and display the **Wastewatchers** logo to welcome the children as they arrive and are registered. As this is the last day, make

sure there is an air of celebration! The children are given their badge for the day and go to their Taskforce Groups. This is an opportunity for Taskforce Leaders to get to review what the children think of the whole club so far, especially the Bible stories and what they have found out in the Bible discovery sections. Can anyone remember the *Learn and Remember verse*(s)?

Taskforce Groups

What you need

- More junk for your model, sitcky tape, scissors or
- Felt-tip pens and the giant rubbish picture (page 54)
- If you planted seeds in Day 1, talk about their progress

Each group should spend time together finishing their giant rubbish picture or junk model. Any children who have brought jokes, pictures or questions should drop them in the bottle bank for the final time.

ON THE TIP
35 minutes

The Binmen/women welcome the children to **Wastewatchers**. If children have been making junk models, now is the best time to put them on display and acknowledge the creativity of the children. Anything else that has been made during the week could be put on display.

Warm up

What you need

- Energetic music and a plan of movements for the children to follow

What you do

Lead a workout to music with a strong beat. The purpose of this is to let the children have fun and use up some energy. As they sit down, ask them what else could have been done to make the tip a nice place to be.

Wastewatchers challenge

Invite four children and four leaders to come to the front for this challenge.

What you need

- Make-up and make-up remover
- Hair bands, ribbons, even silly hats

What you do

Each child has three minutes to make up the head of a leader so that they look as happy as possible! This should produce great hilarity. If you have a digital or video camera, record the process and the results!

Songs

Sing the **Wastewatchers** song. Also sing other non-confessional songs, suitable to use with children who know little about Jesus.

Tell the story

Show Episode 5 from the DVD, in which Jesus meets Mary and she is filled with joy as a result. Alternatively, tell the story from John 20:1–18 in the following way. Older children may have already looked at the first part of the story on the previous day but there is no harm in repeating it.

What you need

- Five large tear-shapes made into faces with the following expressions: anxious/wide-eyed, puzzled, very sad/tearful, questioning, joyful (if you have a capable artist, they can draw them as you speak)

What you do

Tell the story of Mary's visit to the tomb and garden, using these five faces as props. For the fifth expression, you could turn the third one upside down so that it is not tear-shaped. Emphasise that Mary realised Jesus was not dead, but truly alive. Go on to explain briefly how Jesus met with his friends for over a month but then went back to heaven to be with God his Father. In his place he sent the Holy Spirit, who is God everywhere.

That means that God can be with us, wherever we are, whatever we are doing, whoever we are with. (It is important that children understand something of the Ascension and Pentecost.) His friends were no longer sad, because they knew Jesus could be with them. Wow!

Find the WasteWatcherWord (WWW)

Sadness to joy

What you need

- A smiley stamp and ink pad
- Clothes pegs
- The letters of the WWW on separate sheets of paper
- A long skipping rope or piece of paper made into a horizontal S (see diagram – you may need help to support this shape)

What you do

The children take turns in guessing the letters. Every child who guesses correctly gets a smiley stamp on their hand and the letter is pegged onto the S ('SADNESS' to the left and 'JOY' to the right with 'TO' in the middle).

 **TASKFORCE**
50 minutes

Refreshments

5 minutes

Serve the children their refreshments in small groups. Since this is the last day, you may wish to have something special to eat or drink or to serve the refreshments in a special way, eg drinks with bendy straws, hot cross buns.

Bible discovery
15 minutes

With older children

If you are using *Little Green Pages* turn to page xx, or have enough copies of John 20:11–18 for each child. If you're not using *Little Green Pages* you will need at least three teardrops to be made into faces for each child – see the retold story suggestion above. (If you read from verse 1, you will need more than three teardrops.) As you read the story, let the children fill in their teardrops with the emotions Mary is feeling.

With younger children

Give out the Ecdo Sheet. Read out loud John 20:11–18 and ask the children to fill in Mary's face after you have read. You may want to put in the eyes and eyebrows beforehand. What was Mary's face like when she discovered that this was Jesus she was talking to? He was alive! Complete the Eco Sheets.

With all children

Explore the story by adapting the questions below to suit your group:

- When have the children been really sad? Share your own sad experience. Be prepared for a whole range of answers.
- What stopped them/you being sad?
- What stopped Mary being sad?
- If Jesus is still alive and with us, by his Spirit, as was explained earlier, what does that mean for the children in practical ways? (He is with them in the playground, in the classroom, when they are scared, happy, moving to a new school etc.)
- Share your own experience of Jesus' light that gives life, if you have not done that already.
- If appropriate, talk about how we can follow Jesus, using the commitment booklet for the appropriate age.

Pray together. Go round each child inviting them to finish this sentence as they talk with God. You could pass round an object such as a cross and

the children pray when they're holding the object:
'Thank you, Jesus, that you are alive. Thank you that you are with me _____ (in the playground, in bed, in the bath etc).'

Games
15 minutes

The idea of the games today is to have as much fun as possible! Play the games again that have gone the best during the club. You might use a parachute or borrow some play equipment from a local school or let the children just have fun on their own or in small groups. Alternatively, you could bring in some board games which many children rarely play and can be a real treat. Having fun with sympathetic adults is something some children don't often experience. Make sure the leaders join in with these activities!

> For some weeks, the opportunity to play a game of very large snakes and ladders was the reason why several children were always early for my Sunday group! And if you are playing snakes and ladders, you could naturally talk about the snake story from the last session.

Craft
15 minutes

As you do the craft, encourage the children to ask questions about the club or share their reflections about it. The craft today reflects something of the joy of the resurrection!

Musical instruments

What you need

- Any materials to make junk musical instruments

What you do

There are various ways to make musical instruments from junk: plastic bottle/yogurt pot shakers, paper stretched across the top of a round container, coconut shells, claves made from old bits of wood, a decorated 'bumpy' plastic bottle to rub a stick against, bits of sandpaper on a board to rub together, cellophane to scrunch up – anything that makes a noise! The children can use these instruments to join in the final episode of the drama.

Party hats

What you need

• Materials to make your chosen hat designs

What you do

Provide models of a variety of hats and material to make them. Feathers, sticky paper and plenty of glue will make every hat different. Older children will create some sophisticated designs!

Other craft ideas

• A resurrection garden – a popular craft and very appropriate for the story. Provide the children with stones, moss, three crosses and a plant which could be planted in a decorated pot.
• Mini pompoms made from doubled up wool – two circles of card with a hole in the middle are put together, and wool is taken through the hole again and again until the hole disappears. Tie tightly in the middle as you cut through the edge of the circle to release the wool.

In a trial both boys and girls enjoyed making the pompoms, especially as they used the colours of the local football team. They are something visual to wave at the end of the drama.

 **BIG CLEAN UP**
30 minutes

Bottle bank

Sing one or two songs as the children arrive and read out any suitable jokes, display pictures and answer any questions from the bottle bank.

Quiz

Keep your quiz short and snappy with a few questions to review the whole programme, including all the WWW's. Score by letting off a party-popper every time a question is correctly answered. (Be aware of children who may be frightened by noises like this) End by asking what today's WWW is – from sadness to joy!

This happened to me...

Invite a team member to be interviewed or to share their story of why Jesus being alive matters to them, with a further challenge to become a friend or follower of Jesus. Make sure that what they say about Jesus is simple, in child-friendly language and uses the phrases about being in a relationship with God that you have been using all this session. Read pages 30–31 for more suggestions.

Learn and remember

Revise John 8:12 or all the *Learn and remember verses* you have had during the club.

Light experiment

Bring out all three plants and see if the light has made a difference to the growth of the three plants. If it has, you have created a clear way for the children to remember what it means that Jesus is light for the world. If there is no difference, that is the nature of science experiments!

Drama

The drama runs into a time of celebration – the grand opening of the park! You will need to have prepared either the musical instruments or pompoms that the children have made or some already available, including saucepan lid cymbals, homemade shakers etc. The drama demonstrates that the three young people have helped to transform the park into a place that is welcome to everyone. This is a cause for celebration!

Creative prayer idea

We can talk with God by speaking but also by singing. Choose a few songs which celebrate the fact that Jesus is alive – for example 'Sing a song, sing a joyful song (Celebrate)' by Mark and Helen Johnson, *Sing-along Praise and Worship-Songs for Children* CD, Kevin Mayhew Publishers. This song has the refrain: 'Jesus is alive you know, he's risen from the dead, he was crucified but now he's risen as he said, alleluia!' Let the children dance around and, if you have musical instruments, let them play them.

 **TASKFORCE TOO**
5 minutes

Spend the last five minutes of the club in Taskforce Groups, finishing off any craft or puzzles from *Little Green Pages*. Taskforce Leaders should take this opportunity to chat about the whole club. What do they think of the transforming Jesus?
Taskforce Leaders should also make sure they know how each child is getting home. As each child is leaving, make sure they and their parents or carers know about the follow-up service, if you are having one.

FINAL CLEAR UP

Find time to talk together and evaluate the whole programme. When you come to do a fuller review, some of the immediate impressions will have been lost! Is there anyone who needs particular attention and follow-up?

Many churches have a final event that includes parents or carers and may include food. It may also include a final service – see pages 92–93. This is a great opportunity to get to know families better, give parents/carers an opportunity to thank you for caring for their children for the week and make sure everyone knows what is planned for the coming weeks and months.

From sadness to joy

eco sheet

5

"Mary Magdalene stood crying outside the tomb...she turned around and saw Jesus standing there ... She thought he was the gardener and said, 'Sir, if you have taken his body away, please tell me, so I can go and get him.' Then Jesus said to her, 'Mary!'"
John 20:11,14–16

Draw Mary's face when she thought Jesus was the gardener.
Draw Mary's face when she knew Jesus was alive.

Think of places where you go. Write them in the space in this speech bubble.

'Thank you Jesus that you are alive. Thank you that you are with me...

Only two of these pictures are exactly the same. Which ones are they? Colour them all.

Sunday service 2

Aim of this service

- To round up the holiday club programme
- To remind children of what they have discovered over the week
- To help parents, carers and church members share in the Wastewatchers experience.

ALL-AGE SERVICE OUTLINE

Introduction

If possible, split the church (or wherever you meet) in half with one side looking beautiful and the other more tip-like and untidy. Introduce some of the rubbish that was on the tip at the start of **Wastewatchers**. As people are welcomed, invite them to sit on the 'tip side' or the 'transformed side'. Use these two phrases intentionally.

Begin by explaining that **Wastewatchers** began with a beautiful world that God had made but things began to go wrong very soon and the tip was created.

Song

Sing a song to celebrate the beauty of God's world. 'All things bright and beautiful' may be old but it is better known by many parents who do not usually come to church. This will help them feel more comfortable.

Prayer

Ask the children to put their hands up to call out all the beautiful things that God has made. Write them down so all can see. You could replay the presentation you used on Day 1. If you can, arrange for two children to read prayers of thanks to God for his world.

This happened to me…

Interview a leader and a child to say what have been the best things about **Wastewatchers** (you will need to prepare them beforehand carefully).

Songs

Sing some of the songs you have sung during the club including the **Wastewatchers** song.

Quiz

Write a quiz which tests the knowledge of the children (and adults) in terms of what they remember about what happened and also what they remember of the teaching, including the WWW and the *Learn and remember verse*. As you run through the week, talk about how the tip came to be transformed and how so many things have changed!

Keep the quiz fast-moving and score by giving each child/adult with a right answer either a yellow or a red flower shape and ask them to stand up. At the end are there more red or yellow flowers? This is quite arbitrary but avoids having to divide up into teams. Everyone with a flower can keep it!

Bible discovery

Peter was feeling rubbish! (This is a deliberate use of the word 'rubbish' with a meaning that has not been used this week.) Why? He had let down his best friend Jesus. He had said he would never leave Jesus but when it came to it, when Jesus was arrested, Peter had been like everyone else. He had let Jesus down.

But then, after Jesus had died, he came alive again! Peter was really confused now, as well as feeling rubbish! How could he ever look Jesus in the face? How could he ever forgive himself?

Invite some good readers to read John 21:1–19 as a narrative with different people taking the parts. As the story is read, group leaders can act out the roles. When Peter and Jesus draw away from the others, interrupt to ask how Peter must have been feeling.

Jesus has shown that he had forgiven Peter for letting him down. He still loved him. Peter was so thrilled! Suddenly everything had changed – he wasn't rubbish after all! And Jesus had given him a job to do, to follow him and to look after the people who Jesus loved. Peter was transformed. Wow!

(If it is possible, ask everyone on the 'tip side' of the church to move to sit on the 'transformed side'. You could add extra seats during the service if you think this is going to be possible. The upheaval will certainly help people remember this service!)

We are all gathered on the transformed side of the building. That is how God wants us to be (not meaning being squashed!), but leaving behind the rubbish in our lives, which we have referred to as the darkness throughout **Wastewatchers**. Only because of Jesus' death and coming alive again is it possible for us to be forgiven and to get rid of the rubbish in our lives. The dark rubbish is everything that we know is not good and does not please God. Jesus came

as light for the world to give light that gives life. This is not just a message for the children and adults who have been part of **Wastewatchers** but to everyone here!
(Let people know what Alpha-type courses and follow up events are planned.)

This happened to me...

Interview a team member who briefly talks about how much they have enjoyed **Wastewatchers** and what it means to them that they have been forgiven.

Community project

God also wants us to make a difference to his world by doing things to help the environment. As we are transformed, so God wants us to transform the world around us. God told the first people to look after the world, and that's still true today. Fill in the details of what you have done this week in the community project.

Response

Ask everyone to join in the following prayer by saying the words in bold:
God you made the world to be a beautiful place but we have spoilt it.
God forgive us and bless us.
God, you asked people to care for the world, a beautiful world, but we have not done what you asked.
God forgive us and bless us.
God we want to do what we can to care for this world. Show us what we can do and help others join in too.
God forgive us and bless us.
Amen.

Thank people for coming to the service and being part of **Wastewatchers** and thank the team of helpers at **Wastewatchers**. Be careful not to miss anyone out if you are mentioning specific names.

Song

Conclude with a song everyone knows or a favourite from the club. You could sing the **Wastewatchers** song once more.

An alternative theme for this service

Explore the idea of the new creation, looking forward to the time when there will be no more suffering or pain, when the damaged creation will be restored. Focus on Revelation 21:1–4; 22:1–5. Here are a number of suggestions:

Review the beauty of God's world from Day 1.

Tell the story of how the man and woman chose to disobey and how everything started to go wrong.

Talk about the importance of the need to work to protect the environment.

Read the verses in Revelation 21. Putting the verses in chapter 21 into sign language is a wonderful way to help people begin to interpret them. Let people make up their own signs. (One child wanted to act out putting on her slippers and slouching in an armchair because she said, 'That was how God would make his home with us.') Comment on the place of light in chapter 22 and talk about how Jesus is the light for the world.

If you can get hold of it, show the last episode of the video *Megaquest* (SU), a holiday club published by SU in 2000, in which the last episode is based on this passage.

Review what has happened during the club as above.

You will not want to introduce many new songs, but the song 'There's a place' by Paul Oakley (*Spring Harvest 99*) is about the new heaven, although you may think it puts words into people's mouths that they may not be able to say truthfully.

PART

7

What next?

HOW ENVIRONMENTALLY AWARE IS YOUR CHURCH?

Running a **Wastewatchers** programme may raise lots of environmental issues in your church community. One organisation which will help you with this is Eco Congregation (www.EcoCongregation.org) encouraging churches to weave creation into their life and mission. Formally established in 2000 (and 2001 in Scotland) it provides a churches' environmental check- up/audit to help churches identify existing good practice and prioritise areas for development.

For example:

How often in a year are environmental concerns included in worship or programmes for adults, children and youth?

• How does a church demonstrate care for the environment in the way the buildings are cared for? Good use of energy supplies (choosing environmentally responsible energy suppliers), using draft excluders, photocopiers not left on stand-by, dripping taps checked etc.

• Does the church regard its land and grounds as God's land and do everything it can to be a responsible steward of creation? Eg. Wildlife-friendly churchyards,

encouraging wildlife and rainfall collection, by not concreting land for car-parking provision.

• How does the church demonstrate an awareness of fairtrade issues? Supporting Fairtrade organisations and buying Fairtrade products even if it costs more; choosing an ethical bank (for example, the Co-op and Triodos banks).

A Rocha

Supporting A Rocha UK, who helped SU develop this programme, is a very good way of showing your church's commitment to creation care. For over 20 years, A Rocha has studied God's Word and cared for God's world. Currently, A Rocha works on diverse conservation projects in over fifteen countries around the world.

A Rocha can:

• share what the Bible says about tending and keeping God's world

• point to reliable environmental information

• connect like-minded people with each other

• help people make a change for good: to lifestyle, in practical 'creation-care' projects at home and abroad and in tackling the causes and effects of climate change

FOLLOW-UP IDEAS

Wastewatchers needn't finish when your holiday club does. Why not have a midweek **Wastewatchers** club, or one on a Saturday morning? Or you could use the midweek follow-up club to **Wastewatchers** to introduce children to your existing weekly clubs.

High Five

High Five is an eight-session midweek club programme based on social justice issues, developed with the Salvation Army. Part of the *eye level* clubs range, *High Five* has been written for use with children with little or no church background. Others in the range include *Streetwise*, *Clues2Use* and *Rocky Road*. *Awesome!* is an *eye level* club programme based on passages from John, and can also be used to follow up **Wastewatchers**. For more details, visit www.scriptureunion.org.uk/eyelevel

Other kinds of clubs

A midweek, after-school Wastewatchers club

This could be held on school premises or in a church hall or community centre. If you meet immediately after school, consider the following:

- The children will need to unwind from the school day and they will need refreshments.
- Most children will not want to do any school-type activities such as worksheets.
- You might use leaders who do not work 9 to 5.
- If you meet in a school, you are unlikely to attract children from other schools, but you may attract children who did not come to **Wastewatchers**.
- If you meet in a school, you will need to get the permission of parents and the cooperation of school staff.

If you meet later in the evening, bear in mind:

- The children will have had a chance to recover from the school day and they will be ready for some fun and to spend time with others.
- Some children will have homework/reading.
- You will have different leaders available.
- There is an opportunity to talk to parents when they collect their children and even scope for an occasional parents' evening.

A Saturday/Sunday morning Wastewatchers club

- Some children have very busy weekends, especially if they visit a parent with whom they do not live.
- Children are unlikely to be tired or distracted.
- The club can run for a longer time, with scope to do more adventurous activities.
- Leaders who are not available on weekdays may be available for involvement in the club.
- It could more easily be a monthly club.

- Choose the time that best suits everyone – even early Sunday morning or early Sunday evening!

A Wastewatchers cell group

For children who have shown particular interest and want to discover more. *So, Why God?* (SU) would be ideal for this.

OTHER IDEAS

- Stay in touch with the children by personally delivering Christmas and Easter cards.
- Plan a carol service with **Wastewatchers** children in mind.
- For ideas of other celebratory and social events for children outside the church, get hold of *Christmas Wrapped Up!*, *Easter Cracked* and *Celebrations Sorted* – visit the Scripture Union website to find out more details.

- Plan an event as an alternative to Halloween.

Consider working with your local primary school

- You could provide It's Your Move!, the book for children moving on to secondary school, or Get Ready Go!, for children starting school.
- You could offer to take an assembly or RE lesson, or help out in any other way. Primary schools usually welcome suitable adult help.

£5 OFF!

BUY £60 WORTH OF EXTRA WASTEWATCHERS RESOURCES AND GET £5 OFF!

1 Take to your local Christian Bookshop
2 Send to Scripture Union Mail Order, PO Box 5148, Milton Keynes MLO, MK2 2YX with your order and payment
3 Visit our online shop at www.scriptureunion.org.uk and place your order online where the £5 discount will be applied

Working with families

Children, of course, are part of a much wider family network. If we want to see children grow in their faith in Jesus, we need to recognise that family members may not always understand, or sympathise with, the teaching and purpose of any outreach to children. However, they themselves need to talk about a need to know Christ too!

- Make sure that family members are well informed about what has happened during the club and also that they know what is planned in the weeks to come.
- Use some of the ideas in **Wastewatchers** to build good relationships with the family.
- Parenting courses, a men's and women's breakfast, or holiday clubs for the elderly are just some examples of meeting genuine adult needs and building relationships.
- Some family members may be ready for a more specifically Christian exploration or discipleship event/course.
- Older siblings who have attended a holiday club in the past often feel nostalgic when a local holiday club is running. Is this a short-lived opportunity to build bridges?

For more details see Top Tips: Growing Faith with Families (SU) 2007

And finally…

How has your team of leaders developed over the period of the holiday club? Did obvious training needs become apparent?

- Consider setting up a training session (or more than one) to develop the abilities of the team. You could open this out to other churches in your area. There may already be training events in your area – contact SU for further details.
- Encourage your holiday club prayer group to keep praying, updating them regularly.
- Identify any gaps in the leadership of your regular children's programme and invite **Wastewatchers** team members to get involved.

Many holiday clubs are the key time in the year when children's workers are at their most creative and most daring! It would be impossible to sustain that level of activity for the rest of the year but the same spirit of risk and innovation could be sustained! Dream dreams and see what God makes happen!

This voucher cannot be exchanged for cash or any other merchandise and cannot be used with any other offer. This offer includes the **Wastewatchers** resource book, DVD and *Little Green Pages* (singles and packs). It does not include CPO publicity merchandise. Only single orders of £60 and above qualify for this offer.

TO THE RETAILER: Please accept this voucher as a discount payment.

CREDIT DUE: £5.00 less normal trade discount.

This voucher must be returned to:

STL Customer Services, PO Box 300,

Carlisle, Cumbria, CA3 0QS by 3rd September 2007.

NAME OF SHOP: _____

STL ACCOUNT NUMBER: _____

VOWWHC